THE POWER OF POSITIVE CONFESSION

*Moving you from glory to glory with 62 powerful
Bible-based commentaries and confessions...
See amazing victories in just one month!*

I0167410

Ebenezer Nfor

KINGDOM BOOKS

Published by Kingdom Books, an imprint of *CreativeJuicesBooks, Singapore (www.creativejuicesbooks.com)*

National Library Board, Singapore Cataloguing-in-Publication Data

Name(s): Nfor, Ebenezer.
Title: The power of positive confession / Ebenezer Nfor.
Description: Singapore : Kingdom Books, [2019]
Identifier(s): OCN 1126673974 | ISBN 978-981-14-3669-7 (paperback)
Subject(s): LCSH: Christianity--Prayers and devotions. | Christian life.
Classification: DDC 242.2--dc23

Contents

Acknowledgments

I wish to express my appreciation to all who have contributed to make this work a reality. First, I thank Jesus for the inspiration and grace to produce this work. Special thanks also go to my wife—my angel, Rosaline Kertain Nfor—and our dearly beloved children: Mishael, Joel and James.

I would also like to express my indebtedness to the producers of Power Bible for making this resource available. Thanks to all who helped in the proofreading too.

Special thanks go to Ursula Lang and her team for their tireless efforts to edit, proofread and publish this book. Dear woman of God, may the Almighty God, our LORD Jesus Christ, multiply His blessings on you. *Hebrews 6:10* says:

"For God is not unrighteous to forget your work and labour of love, which ye have shewed toward His name, in that ye have ministered to the saints, and do minister."

May God richly bless you all!

With Love,
Pastor Ebenezer Bimi Nfor
God's Divine Assembly
Douala, Cameroon, Africa
Tel. (237) 677 97 23 54 /
(237) 698 12 31 56
Email: ebenezernfor@gmail.com

Introduction

Death and life are in the power of the tongue: and they that love it shall eat the fruit thereof.

Proverbs 18:21

For he that will love life, and see good days, let him refrain his tongue from evil, and his lips that they speak no guile.

1 Peter 3:10

Whether we like it or not, our lives will go in the direction of our tongues. The words we speak are seed, and every seed planted brings with it a harvest. Good words planted will bring a good harvest; bad words planted will bring a bad harvest.

You are what you are today because of the words you spoke yesterday. You will become tomorrow what you are speaking today. So, plant God's Word, speak it into your life. It has power to produce a good harvest. As Paul said:

I am not ashamed of the gospel of Christ: for it is the **power of God** unto salvation to everyone that believeth; to the Jew first, and also to the Greek.

Romans 1:16

Positive confession (declaration) of God's Word will bring about positive results in your life, but only if it is accompanied by faith; for, without faith, it is impossible to please God (*Hebrews 11:6*). Jesus tells us:

Verily I say unto you, If ye have **faith**, and doubt not... if ye shall **say** unto this mountain, be thou removed, and be thou cast into the sea; it shall be done.

Matthew 21:21

1

God gave Joshua the secret to a successful life. Many times, we are tempted to blame God or others for where we are in life. But, according to what God told Joshua, He has done all He needs to do to make us successful. He has given us a bag of seed—His Word. It is left to us to determine our level of success, as we apply the principles that He has revealed to us in His Word. This is what God told Joshua:

> This book of the law shall not depart out of thy **mouth**; but thou shalt **meditate** (*hagah*) therein **day and night**, that thou mayest **observe** to do according to all that is written therein: for then thou shalt **make** thy way prosperous, and then thou shalt have good success.
>
> *Joshua 1:8*

The Hebrew word for "meditate" here is *hagah*, which means to mutter, to speak, to talk, to utter, to roar. It is all about making heartfelt declarations, day and night, in conjunction with what God has said. Your confession must flow from your heart: for "out of the abundance of the heart the mouth speaketh" (*Matthew 12:34*).

If God says I am blessed, then I say I am blessed. If He says I am rich, then I say I am rich. If He says I am righteous, then I am righteous. I don't have to feel blessed to be blessed. Neither do I need to feel rich to be rich, or feel righteous to be righteous.

What matters is what God says, not what I feel or think or see, or what others think about me or say about me. When God appeared to Gideon, Gideon saw himself as a "nobody". But God called him a "mighty man of valour" (*Judges 6:12*). And what a mighty man of valour he did turn out to be!

> God, who quickeneth the dead, and **calleth** those things which be not as though they were.
>
> *Romans 4:17*

Proverbs 23:7 tells us that, as a man thinks in his heart, so is he. Your thinking is shaped by what you say, and what you say depends on what you have laid up in your heart. Paul, writing to the Philippians, said:

> Finally, brethren, whatsoever things are true, whatsoever things are honest, whatsoever things are just, whatsoever things are pure, whatsoever things are lovely, whatsoever things are of good report; if there be any virtue, and if there be any praise, think on these things.
>
> *Philippians 4:8*

Think on "these things"—positive things—as the Spirit of God leads you. Think on them daily. Confess them—declare them with confidence and authority—and see your life turn around!

I must warn you, though: this is not a magic wand that you wave to get a desired outcome; it is simply learning to stand on the promises of God by faith.

When you confess God's Word aloud, your way of thinking will change. And your changed way of thinking will change your way of acting, which in turn will result in a positive change in your life—to the glory of God!

For God to work in your life, however, you must yield to Him. You must become a child of God. You must be born again, like Jesus told Nicodemus: "Verily, verily, I say unto thee, except a man be born again, he cannot see the kingdom of God" (*John 3:3*).

You must accept that God loves you and has a wonderful plan for your life (*John 10:10; 3:16*). You must accept that you have sinned and fallen short of the glory of God and that the payment for your sins is death (*Romans 3:23; 6:23*). You must accept that the only way you can be reconciled with God is through Jesus (*John 14:6; Romans 5:8*).

You must ask Jesus to come into your life, forgive your sins, make you a child of God, and give you eternal life (*John 1:12; 1 John 5:11-13; Revelation 3:20*). You must be willing to be baptized in Jesus' Name, so that your sins may be forgiven. Then you will receive the gift of the Holy Spirit (*Acts 2:36-39*).

If you have never invited Jesus Christ into your life and would like to do so, simply pray this prayer:

> Lord Jesus, I acknowledge You as my Lord and my God. I acknowledge You as the Christ, the Son of the Living God. I repent of all my sins. I ask You to come into my life, to take control of my life, and to make me a new person. I believe in my heart that You died for my sins and rose again. Fill me with Your Holy Spirit and help me to live for You daily. In Jesus' Name, Amen.

If you said that prayer sincerely, be assured that Jesus has come into your life, as He promised. He will never leave you nor forsake you. Talk with Him daily through prayer, and meditate and act upon His Word (the Bible) daily.

You will also need to fellowship with others who have surrendered their lives to Christ: ask the Holy Spirit to lead you where Jesus is adored in Spirit and in Truth, and where His Word is preached and studied.

May you be blessed as you confess God's Word until it takes hold of you and makes you what you ought to be—for the glory of God, as we await the soon-coming return of Christ.

This book is not meant to replace the Bible; rather, it is intended to motivate you to love God's Word even more. Be blessed as you allow His Word to transform your life and make you, in turn, an instrument of transformation in the lives of others. I will be delighted to hear from you about the impact the Word of God has had on your life. *Shalom!*

I am too talented to stagnate

And unto one he gave five talents[1], to another two, and to another one; to every man according to his several ability.

Matthew 25:15

God has given each one of us different talents. We do not have to envy others or complain about what we don't have. There should be no room in our hearts for bitterness, and no excuse for laziness either. All we need to do is ask God to reveal to us what our talents are and how to develop and use them. As we develop and use our talents for God's glory, our lives will be blessed, and we will become a blessing to others too.

There was once a widow who was left indebted when her husband died. She thought she had nothing; but there was "a pot of oil" in her house (*2 Kings 4:2*). There is always "a pot of oil" we have been neglecting, always something we considered too insignificant to have any value at all—like the five loaves of bread and two fishes that Jesus multiplied (*John 6:1-14*). But God is in the business of taking what we despise, blessing it, breaking it, and blessing the multitudes with it!

Repeat this confession as many times as you can; as you go through each day, no matter what obstacles you face, remind yourself that...

IN JESUS' NAME, I AM TOO GIFTED AND TALENTED TO STAGNATE!

---

[1] A talent was about 16-20 years' pay for a typical laborer in those days.

I walk in wisdom because the Wonderful Counsellor lives in me

For unto us a child is born, unto us a son is given: and the government shall be upon his shoulder: and his name shall be called *Wonderful, Counsellor*... mighty God, The everlasting Father, The Prince of Peace.

Isaiah 9:6

Wisdom is the principal thing; therefore get wisdom: and with all thy getting get understanding.

Proverbs 4:7

Wisdom is not just a gift or a thing or a spirit. Depending on the context, wisdom can be a person too. In *Proverbs 4:1-13*, Wisdom is personified as a "she" because of her capacity to beautify a man's life. In Colossians, Christ is called the Wisdom of God: "Christ; in whom are hid all the treasures of wisdom and knowledge" (*Colossians 2:2-3*). Also, one of the seven spirits of God is called the spirit of wisdom:

> And there shall come forth a rod out of the stem of Jesse, and a Branch shall grow out of his roots: and the spirit of the LORD shall rest upon him, the **spirit of wisdom** and understanding, the spirit of counsel and might, the spirit of knowledge and of the fear of the LORD...
>
> *Isaiah 11:1-2*

He who does not have Christ in him is foolish. The Bible says it clearly: "The fool hath said in his heart, there is no God"

6

(*Psalm 14:1*); but "the fear of the LORD is the beginning of wisdom" (*Proverbs 9:10*). When the Word of God describes Jesus not only as Counsellor, but Wonderful Counselor, it is because in Him are deposited ALL the treasures of wisdom and knowledge. If Christ Jesus is in you, you have a Wonderful Counsellor living in you. You have the greatest Adviser, the best Life Coach living in you.

You have someone who can give you the answer to every question, the solution to every problem you will ever face; someone who can direct you to make the right decisions, show you the path of life. Someone who can counsel you on who to marry, how to live with your spouse, how to bring up your children, what kind of business to do (see *Genesis 26:12-14*). Even where to stay. Which school to attend. Which career to choose. When to travel and when not to. How to go about the ministry He has given you. Because He is a Wonderful Counsellor, He will give you only the best counsel. You cannot fail if you follow His advice.

You need to consult Jesus before making any decision. Sad to say, most so-called children of God do not do this, even when making major decisions. Many choose to confide in man instead. Some make an outward show of consulting God, but they have already have made their own decisions and are just trying to lure God, to get Him to buy into their decision. This often happens with Christians who decide to marry non-Christians, knowing full well it is not God's will for His children to be unequally yoked with unbelievers (*2 Corinthians 6:14*). But they try to appease their conscience by assuring themselves that the unbelieving spouse will eventually be saved.

On the other hand, many Christians truly desire to consult God and know His will for their lives, but they do not know how to go about it. What we need to do is to spend time alone with Him. Discerning God's will requires intimacy with Him.

We need to seek Him in prayer and study His Word. God will never ask us to do anything contrary to His Word. He can speak to us through the Bible or direct us through circumstances He places in our lives (*Psalm 139:5*). He can also guide us through the counsel of godly men and women: "For by wise counsel thou shalt make thy war: and in multitude of counsellors there is safety" (*Proverbs 24:6*). When the decision we make is in line with God's will, we will often feel an inner peace about it.

Peter and his friends laboured all night and caught no fish (*Luke 5:1-7*). But, when Jesus showed up and they obeyed His instructions, they got an amazing catch. What the Wonderful Counsellor did for them, He can do for you too. Have you been labouring all night, with nothing to show for it? Jesus can change your story. Only be willing to seek Him and do as He tells you. You will get amazing results, as His followers did.

He says, "My sheep hear my voice, and I know them, and they follow me" (*John 10:27*). When you follow Jesus, you will never be a failure. Even if you do fall, don't give up; you will surely succeed in the end. *Proverbs 24:16* says: "For a just man falleth seven times, and riseth up again: but the wicked shall fall into mischief." What you call failure is only a life lesson the Lord might be teaching you. All the great inventors never got it the first time. They succeeded because they persevered.

At first, you might struggle to discern the Lord's voice. But as you persevere, all will work out well for you. With the Wonderful Counsellor in you, you will make the right decisions. You will become a star and a consultant to others. The more you lean on Jesus, the more you will move from success to success, from glory to glory; just like *Proverbs 4:18* says: "But the path of the just is as the shining light, that shineth more and more unto the perfect day." Simply declare:

I WALK IN WISDOM BECAUSE THE WONDERFUL COUNSELLOR LIVES IN ME!

I am too blessed to be fruitless

And God blessed them, and God said unto them, Be fruitful, and multiply, and replenish the earth, and subdue it: and have dominion over the fish of the sea, and over the fowl of the air, and over every living thing that moveth upon the earth.

Genesis 1:28

God will never ask us to do what He has not enabled us to do. To be blessed is to be enabled or uplifted or exhorted. What this means is that God is on our side every day, cheering us on and enabling us to do all He has commanded us to do.

Fruitfulness is a command. To be fruitful is to grow, to increase, to bring forth a bountiful result. To multiply is to increase greatly, to grow or produce abundantly, to exceed. To replenish is to fill to the top, to overflow, to get to fullness. To subdue is to conquer. Paul says "we are more than conquerors through him [Jesus] that loved us" (*Romans 8:37*). To dominate is to rule or reign. You were born to reign over the circumstances of life:

> For if by one man's offence death reigned by one; much more they which receive abundance of grace and of the gift of righteousness shall reign in life by one, Jesus Christ.

> *Romans 5:17*

If you have fallen, get up and keep going. Never start a day with a defeatist mentality. Your projects might have failed, but you are not a failure.

9

Those around you might be shouting, "You cannot make it!" Don't give in to their negativism. If you are a child of God, He is on your side. He is exhorting you now to be all He created you to be. You are more than able to do so.

It is important to note that God never blessed man to have dominion over other men, but over His creation. To seek to dominate over your fellow human being is to go against God's plan. To seek to dominate over God's creation is to bring glory to God and be a source of blessing to others. Outside of God's plan, there is no blessing:

> Except the LORD build the house, they labour in vain that build it: except the LORD keep the city, the watchman waketh but in vain.
>
> *Psalm 127:1*

Some have asked: "If God's will for us is dominion, why is life so harsh at times?" Instead of domination over God's creation, we may find ourselves dominated by circumstances—poverty, sickness, failure, and much more. Why? The answer is: *because of sin.* From the time man disobeyed God, he compromised his ability to dominate over creation (see *Genesis 3:17-19*).

The ground became cursed because of the wrong choice he made: from thenceforth, he would have to wrest a living from the soil. But thank God that, with the coming of Christ, the story has changed. Putting our faith in Christ's finished work on the cross, we can again have dominion over creation.

Because Jesus is the Lord of your life, you can declare with confidence:

IN JESUS' NAME,
I AM TOO BLESSED TO BE FRUITLESS!

I am highly protected because the Mighty God lives in me

For unto us a child is born, unto us a son is given: and the government shall be upon his shoulder: and his name shall be called Wonderful, Counsellor, *The mighty God*, The everlasting Father, The Prince of Peace.

Isaiah 9:6

Apart from being your Wonderful Counsellor, Jesus is also your Mighty God. It is important to note that Jesus is not just a god—contrary to what some believe—or even just Mighty God, but that He is also LORD and GOD and ALMIGHTY GOD (*John 20:28; Revelation 1:8*).

The word for "mighty" in Hebrew is *gibbowr*, meaning "powerful"; by implication, it is used to describe a warrior, champion or chief, a strong or valiant man. "Almighty" in Greek is *pantokrator,* which means 'the all-ruling"—that is, God (as absolute, universal and omnipotent Sovereign).

What all this means is that the powerful, all-ruling God of the universe lives in you. Moses called Him "the Rock" (*Deuteronomy 32:4*), and from Paul we have the assurance that He lives in us: "Christ *in* you, the hope of glory" (*Colossians 1:27*); a fact reinforced by the Apostle John's declaration that "greater is he [Jesus] that is *in* you, than he that is in the world" (*1 John 4:4*). Just stop and meditate on this, and all your fears will fade away.

11

You don't have to be afraid of anyone or any situation. The most powerful and all-ruling God lives in you and is ready to fight for you. You are highly protected. You are in good hands. No need to seek protection from psychics or the occult. Those who seek protection outside of God do so out of ignorance.

The Bible tells us that protection from our Almighty God is our heritage:

> No weapon that is formed against thee shall prosper; and every tongue that shall rise against thee in judgment thou shalt condemn. This is the heritage of the servants of the LORD, and their righteousness is of me, saith the LORD.
>
> *Isaiah 54:17*

In the battles of life, we need to let God fight for us, for the battle is His (*1 Samuel 17:47; 2 Chronicles 20:15*). Our fight is not physical but spiritual (*Ephesians 6:12*). All we need is to take our positions, and God will fight through us and for us and give us victory, like He did for Joshua (*Joshua 1:5*), David (*1 Samuel 17:46-50*), Jehoshaphat (*2 Chronicles 20:14-30*), and many more.

You are more than a conqueror because the Champion of champions lives in you. You can declare with confidence:

I AM HIGHLY PROTECTED BECAUSE THE MIGHTY GOD LIVES IN ME!

DAY 3—MORNING

I am too empowered to fail

But ye shall receive power, after that the Holy Ghost is come upon you: and ye shall be witnesses unto me both in Jerusalem, and in all Judaea, and in Samaria, and unto the uttermost part of the earth.

Acts 1:8

When we get born again, God's Spirit comes and lives in us (*Romans 8:9*). But though we are indwelt by the Holy Spirit, we still need to allow Him to empower and lead us daily. Paul exhorts us, "be not drunk with wine, wherein is excess; but be filled with the Spirit" (*Ephesians 5:18*).

Paul likens the filling of the Holy Spirit to being drunk with wine because, when we are drunk, we are no longer in control of ourselves, but the wine controls us. Similarly, when we are filled with God's Spirit, it is His Spirit who is in control of our lives and who empowers us to do supernatural things.

It was the outpouring of God's Spirit on the early disciples that emboldened Peter to talk about the very Jesus he had denied a few days ago (*Acts 2:14-40*). It is God's Spirit poured out on us that enables us to be the people He wants us to be and to fulfill the assignments He has given us.

Do you ever feel like you lack the energy needed to live a life that honours God and fulfills His assignments for you? Thank God that His Spirit and His anointing are available to help you: "Not by might, nor by power, but by my spirit, saith the LORD of hosts" (*Zechariah 4:6*).

13

All you need to do is to desire to be filled. Then, confess all your sins, yield yourself to God, and ask to be filled by faith. Just as you have received Christ by faith, you are filled with God's Spirit by faith. *Luke 11:13* says:

> If ye then, being evil, know how to give good gifts unto your children: how much more shall your heavenly Father give the Holy Spirit to them that ask Him.

Right now, ask God to fill you with His Holy Spirit as He promised, so that you can honour Him and do the good works He has assigned you to do (*Ephesians 2:10*).

In *John 14:12*, Jesus announced:

> Verily, verily, I say unto you, He that believeth on me, the works that I do shall he do also; and greater works than these shall he do; because I go unto my Father.

What were the works that Jesus did? In *Luke 4:18-19*, He proclaimed:

> The Spirit of the Lord is upon me, because he hath anointed me to preach the gospel to the poor; he hath sent me to heal the brokenhearted, to preach deliverance to the captives, and recovering of sight to the blind, to set at liberty them that are bruised, To preach the acceptable year of the Lord.

Jesus, who lives in you, is an anointed Saviour. *Isaiah 10:27* says that the anointing destroys the yoke. Therefore, because of the unction that you carry, every yoke in and around you will be destroyed: the yokes of sickness, poverty, failure, fear, confusion, fruitlessness, disappointment, discouragement, stagnation, unrighteousness... every bondage, every burden will be destroyed in the Name of Jesus!

As God fills us with His Spirit, He also enables us to manifest different spiritual gifts through which our life's assignments may be accomplished. For more on this, you can read *1 Corinthians 12:1-11, Ephesians 4:11-13, 1 Peter 4:10,* and *Romans 12:6-8.*

Here is a suggested prayer you can pray if you desire to be filled with God's Spirit:

> *Heavenly Father, I come to you in the Name of Jesus. I am sorry for depending on myself to live the Christian life. Please forgive me. Fill me with your Holy Spirit and enable me to live a life that honours you. Help me by your Spirit to understand my life assignment better and to fulfill it as I ought. Let my ministration be backed by the manifestation of the gifts of your Spirit.*
> *In Jesus' Name, Amen.*

As you go through the day, confess this with confidence as many times as possible:

**IN THE NAME OF JESUS,
I AM TOO EMPOWERED TO FAIL!**

My needs are met, for the Everlasting Father dwells in me

For unto us a child is born, unto us a son is given: and the government shall be upon his shoulder: and his name shall be called Wonderful, Counsellor, The mighty God, *The everlasting Father*, The Prince of Peace.

Isaiah 9:6

I remember how my earthly father used to take care of us when we were growing up. He provided adequately for his family, as a good father should. He always bought groceries in bulk—bags of flour, rice, all kinds of foodstuffs for the family. We had everything in abundance. Besides that, he also made sure his children went to good schools and dressed well. When we were sick, he took good care of us. If an earthly father can do all that, how much more will your everlasting heavenly Father?

My father did his best, but today he is no more. On the other hand, once you invite Jesus into your life, He becomes not only your Father and source of provision, but your everlasting source. He will not be here today and gone tomorrow. Everlasting means "perpetually, world without end". You are not an orphan. You can count on Jesus to supply all your needs according to His riches in glory.

Of all the gifts our everlasting Father can give His children, the best one of all is the gift of His Holy Spirit, who comes to live in us and with us.

Jesus has given us this assurance:

> If ye then, being evil, know how to give good gifts unto your children: how much more shall your heavenly Father give the Holy Spirit to them that ask him?
>
> *Luke 11:13*

The Spirit of Christ in us is the best of gifts, because it is through Him that we have access to all the other gifts. It is His Spirit that gives us power to get wealth (*Deuteronomy 8:18*).

Just as we need to ask Him to fill us with His Spirit, we also need to ask Him for everything else we need. God knows our every need, but He wants us to ask Him to meet those needs:

> Ask, and it shall be given you; seek, and ye shall find; knock, and it shall be opened unto you: For every one that asketh receiveth; and he that seeketh findeth; and to him that knocketh it shall be opened.
>
> *Matthew 7:7-8*

Asking is a sign of our dependence on God. It makes Him feel fatherly, that He has children who look up to Him. Imagine a child who never asks anything of his father. The father might easily conclude that that child has another source he is depending on!

Beyond our asking and seeking and knocking, however, our Everlasting Father longs for more... an intimate relationship with us. He does not want our relationship with Him to be limited to asking, seeking and knocking. He wants us to love Him, above all else, for who He is and not for what we can get from Him (*Matthew 22:37*). When we become intimate with God, He will start answering us even before we ask Him.

The story is told of a preacher's son who one day came and stood in his father's study while the man of God was busy preparing his sermon. At one point, the father became nervous because the young man stood beside him for a long time without saying a word. So, the man asked, "Son, what in particular do you want?"

To his great surprise, the son replied, "Daddy, I just want to be in your presence."

How wonderful it would be, if we desire to just spend time with our Heavenly and Everlasting Father! We were created for intimacy with God, but it is sad that most people follow Jesus for the loaves, not because they just love His presence. How intimate are you with Jesus?

The result of intimacy is that we become familiar with the voice of Jesus:

> My sheep hear my voice, and I know them, and they follow me.
>
> *John 10:27*

When we can discern Jesus' voice, we will be able to gain access to His provision and care for us as our Heavenly and Everlasting Father.

Based on these truths, you can declare confidently that:

MY NEEDS ARE MET, FOR THE EVERLASTING FATHER DWELLS IN ME. AMEN!

Greater is He that is in me than he that is in the world

Ye are of God, little children, and have overcome them: because greater is He that is in you, than he that is in the world.

1 John 4:4

Nothing and nobody should ever make you judge yourself by your outward circumstances. The real you is not what is seen physically. Your real identity is drawn from Him who inhabits you. You are created in the image of the Creator God.

God is a Spirit (*John 4:24*). You too are a spirit. You are a spirit that has a soul and lives in a body. When you receive Christ, He comes to dwell in you and gets married to your spirit. No matter what opposition you may face from the outside, the One who is in you is greater and able to take care of it. God is greater than all external forces, for He created all and has control over all.

This knowledge should banish fear from your heart. God has not given us a spirit of fear but of boldness, of love, and of a sound mind (*2 Timothy 1:7*).

The Spirit in you enables you to overcome with boldness every error propagated by the anti-Christ. You have a great Teacher living in you. So, stop running around, seeking help from so-called men of God. The role of men of God is to help you develop intimacy with God, not replace God in your life.

But the anointing which ye have received of him abideth in you, and ye need not that any man teach you: but as the same anointing teacheth you of all things, and is truth, and is no lie, and even as it hath taught you, ye shall abide in him.

1 John 2:27

Because the One in you is a Great Teacher, you must seek to develop intimacy with Him. Then He will enable you to gain victory over error and also help guide others:

For whatsoever is born of God overcometh the world: and this is the victory that overcometh the world, even our faith.

1 John 5:4

When you are faced with challenges, remember that "greater is He that is in you, than he that is in the world" (*1 John 4:4*). Continue to confess this until it takes a hold of you:

GREATER IS HE THAT IS IN ME THAN HE THAT IS IN THE WORLD!

I walk in perfect peace, for the Prince of Peace dwells in me

For unto us a child is born, unto us a son is given: and the government shall be upon his shoulder: and his name shall be called Wonderful, Counsellor, The mighty God, The everlasting Father, *The Prince of Peace.*

Isaiah 9:6

To have Jesus as the Prince (*Sar*) of Peace (*Shalom*) means to have the Master of Prosperity living in you. Peace in this context is more than the absence of war: it speaks of complete wellness; it speaks of wholeness. It speaks of all-round success —in your spiritual life, social life and physical wellbeing, and in your family, finances, ministry, business and career.

So, why are we still anxious, when we have the Master of all-round prosperity living in us? Why is it that, in spite of the presence of Jesus in us, we are often troubled by one thing or another? Jesus said it is the people of the world who worry about what they will eat or drink or wear. He counselled, "But seek ye first the kingdom of God, and His righteousness; and all these things shall be added unto you" (*Matthew 6:33*).

In *Hosea 4:6*, God said of the children of Israel, "My people are destroyed for lack of knowledge." Ignorance is responsible for our often-worried state: ignorance of who we are, whose we are, and who we possess.

We forget who is in us. We forget His promises to us. We are ignorant of His Word—or, if we do know it, we refuse to apply it in our given circumstances. Instead of casting all our cares on Jesus (as *1 Peter 5:7* exhorts us) we choose to carry them, and they end up giving us stress.

No amount of worrying can solve any problem. The more we worry about a problem, the bigger it becomes. The more we focus on Jesus, the smaller the problem becomes, and the bigger Jesus becomes. Problems are opportunities for us to seek God and thereby experience His miracle-working power in our lives. As a popular song goes, "Why worry, when you can pray? Trust in Jesus and He will lead the way."[2]

The following hymn, by Joseph M. Scriven, can also be of encouragement to us:

What a Friend we have in Jesus,
   All our sins and griefs to bear!
What a privilege to carry
   Everything to God in prayer!
O what peace we often forfeit,
   O what needless pain we bear,
All because we do not carry
   Everything to God in prayer!

Are we weak and heavy-laden,
   Cumbered with a load of care?
Precious Savior, still our refuge—
   Take it to the Lord in prayer;
Do thy friends despise, forsake thee?
   Take it to the Lord in prayer;
In His arms He'll take and shield thee,
   Thou wilt find a solace there.

---

[2] *Why Worry When You Can Pray*, by John W. Peterson.

To live worry-free lives and enjoy the peace of God which passes all understanding, we must follow the advice given by Paul in his letter to the Philippians:

> Be careful [*i.e., full of care*3] for nothing; but in everything by prayer and supplication with thanksgiving let your requests be made known unto God. And the peace of God, which passeth all understanding, shall keep your hearts and minds through Christ Jesus.
>
> *Philippians 4:6-7*

Here is a step-by-step guide to applying Paul's advice:

1. Refuse to live a life that is full of care. Stop worrying. Stop asking yourself questions such as... *How will I pay my bills? My rent? My children's school fees? How will I meet deadlines at work? Accomplish this task? That project?*

2. Choose to present all your requests to God (*1 Peter 5:7*).

3. Stay in a spirit of thanksgiving to God, as a sign of faith that He has already answered you (*Romans 4:19*). As you spend time praising God, you give Him an opportunity to work on your case.

4. Allow God to fill you with His peace, which passes all understanding. Stop worrying about how the answer will come or where it will come from. God works in wonderful ways. Stay at peace, and you will receive inspiration and instruction on what to do. God is good all the time.

Most often, we present our requests to God and, after that, we carry them back with us instead of leaving them with Him. This only compounds the problem. We must trust that God hears us and will answer us in His own way and timing. He is always on time with His answers.

---

3 Bracketed words in italics are the author's.

The following scripture verses will help you to stay focused on God and to trust in Him:

> But without faith it is impossible to please him: for he that cometh to God must believe that he is, and that he is a rewarder of them that diligently seek him.
>
> *Hebrews 11:6*

> And this is the confidence that we have in him, that, if we ask any thing according to his will, he heareth us: And if we know that he hear us, whatsoever we ask, we know that we have the petitions that we desired of him.
>
> *1 John 5:14-15*

> Thou wilt keep him in perfect peace, whose mind is stayed on thee: because he trusteth in thee.
>
> *Isaiah 26:3*

Fortified with all these assurances from God's Word, you can declare with confidence:

I WALK IN PERFECT PEACE, FOR THE PRINCE OF PEACE DWELLS IN ME. AMEN!

Christ in me is my hope of a glorious life

To whom God would make known what is the riches of the glory of this mystery among the Gentiles; which is *Christ in you, the hope of glory*.

Colossians 1:27

If you have invited Christ into your life, you are carrying the God of the universe within you. He is no longer far away in heaven. This is a secret that has been revealed to us—because, before Jesus was revealed, man had always seen God as being distant and far away.

Another name for Jesus is Emmanuel, meaning "God with us". When He was asked about God's Kingdom, Jesus said, "Behold, the kingdom of God is within you" (*Luke 17:21*). To have Jesus, therefore, is to have the Kingdom of God inside you.

The Kingdom of God is a glorious Kingdom. It is a Kingdom of righteousness, peace and joy in the Holy Spirit (*Romans 14:17*). Nothing beautiful is lacking in it. The streets are made of gold. It is such a glorious Kingdom that, when we partake of it, we want to share it with others too.

John 7:38 says: "He that believeth on me, as the scripture hath said, out of his belly shall flow rivers of living water." Do you know that you are carrying an inexhaustible "gold mine" inside you? The answers to the world's questions are in you; the solutions to the world's problems are in you. If only we will learn to remove our eyes from our external circumstances and start looking inward! Then life can become really exciting!

The story is often told of a man who bought a ticket for a long sea cruise. Throughout his trip he almost starved, because all he had to eat were a few biscuits he had brought along with him. He could only look on at all the other passengers who were having a good time enjoying the sumptuous meals provided on the ship.

Then the day came when all his biscuits were eaten up. Desperately hungry, he finally worked up the courage to approach one of the hostesses. He asked to be given a job so that he could earn some money to buy food. The hostess was taken aback and asked him, "Haven't you paid for the trip?"

Yes, he had paid for the ticket, was his reply. The hostess then explained to him that his ticket covered all the expenses for the cruise, including all the meals provided on the ship. His ignorance had caused him to miss out on all the good things that could have been his for the taking!

In *Hosea 4:6*, God lamented that His people were being destroyed for lack of knowledge. The greatest poverty is the poverty of the mind. Studies reveal that ninety percent of people find themselves in trouble because they do not know who they are. Until you know what you carry within you, you can never take advantage of it.

There once lived a man who went searching for diamonds all over the world until the day he died. But he never found them. Then, just after his death, diamonds were discovered by his heir in the backyard of his house!

It is time to take advantage of what you carry—Christ in you! With Christ living in you, you are no longer ordinary, but you have become extraordinary. Physically, everything looks the same. But, spiritually, a lot has changed. As you choose to dig deeper into this inner treasure in you, it is only a matter of time when you begin to unpack and enjoy the contents of this inner treasure and become a blessing to the world (*2 Peter 1:3-4; Genesis 12:1-2*).

The Anointed Saviour lives in you 24/7. He assures you, "I will never leave you nor forsake you." (*Hebrews 13:5, NKJV*). When everything around you looks hopeless, it is good to know that you have real hope of a glorious life. The glory of the indwelling Anointed One speaks of His dignity.

To sum it up: because Christ is living in me, I walk in confidence, dignity and all-round wealth. *Colossians 2:3* says that in Christ "are hid all the treasures of wisdom and knowledge". As you go through this day and through life, remember to confess over and over again that:

CHRIST IN ME IS MY HOPE OF A GLORIOUS LIFE!

Because I call upon the Lord, I walk in revelation knowledge

Call unto me, and I will answer thee, and show thee great and mighty things, which thou knowest not.

Jeremiah 33:3

Just when Jeremiah found himself in a tight spot, he received God's promise to show him "great and mighty things", if he called upon Him. God's promise to Jeremiah is also available to us today, but we need not wait until we are in a tight spot before calling upon Him. We are to call upon Him at all times. Of course, in times when we are discouraged and confused and have run out of strategies, then all the more we should call upon Him like never before.

God has promised us, "I will instruct thee and teach thee in the way which thou shalt go: I will guide thee with mine eye" (*Psalm 32:8*). Nothing is as great as divine revelation and direction. The Psalmist proclaimed joyfully: "Thou wilt shew me the path of life: in thy presence is fulness of joy; at thy right hand there are pleasures for evermore" (*Psalm 16:11*).

Are you presently at the crossroads of your life, not knowing what to do? Call upon God.

Are you in a dilemma, with a difficult decision to make, not knowing which option to choose? Call upon God.

Are you facing difficulties in your workplace, marriage, relationships, ministry, finances or other matters, and you don't know what to do? Call upon God.

What does it mean to call upon God? How are we to call upon Him? We need God to help us know how to call upon Him. As it says in His Word:

> Likewise the Spirit also helps in our weaknesses. For we do not know what we should pray for as we ought, but the Spirit Himself makes intercession for us with groanings which cannot be uttered.
>
> *Romans 8:26, NKJV*

To call upon God is to talk to God. But it is not just talking; it is talking *from our hearts*. It is talking with perseverance, refusing to give up until we get His answer. It is asking, seeking and knocking (*Isaiah 62:6-7; Luke 18:1-8; Matthew 7:7-8*). Calling upon God demonstrates our faith in Him and causes us to give Him the glory when His secrets are revealed to us:

> And call upon me in the day of trouble: I will deliver thee, and thou shalt glorify me.
>
> *Psalm 50:15*

The revelations of the Lord bring deliverance. Daniel and his friends understood this truth and made good use of it:

> Then was the secret revealed unto Daniel in a night vision. Then Daniel... said, Blessed be the name of God... he giveth wisdom unto the wise, and knowledge to them that know understanding: he revealeth the deep and secret things... and hast made known unto me now what we desired of thee: for thou hast now made known unto us the king's matter.
>
> *Daniel 2:19-23*

With all this in mind, you can declare with confidence:

BECAUSE I CALL UPON THE LORD, I WALK IN REVELATION KNOWLEDGE!

Whatsoever I do shall prosper

And he shall be like a tree planted by the rivers of water, that bringeth forth his fruit in his season; his leaf also shall not wither; *and whatsoever he doeth shall prosper.*

Psalm 1:3

To prosper is to push forward; to break out; to proceed (mightily); to be good, to be profitable. It also means to be well; to be healthy. Being healthy is not only about being in good physical shape; it is about thriving in all areas of our lives:

> Beloved, I wish above all things that thou mayest prosper and be in health, even as thy soul prospereth.
>
> *3 John 2*

God wants us to be physically, spiritually, emotionally, intellectually, socially and materially well to do. *Psalm 1:1-3* says that, when we meditate on God's Word day and night, whatever we do shall prosper. We shall push forward, proceed mightily in all our endeavours, and do well in everything.

It is sad that prosperity for most people has been reduced to mean only material prosperity. But *Psalm 1:3* does not say we shall prosper in *some* things; it says *whatsoever* we do shall prosper. Neither does it say whatsoever we *wish* shall prosper; it says whatsoever we *do*. James tells us we are not to be hearers only but doers of God's Word (*James 1:22-25*).

When God tells me to do something and I do it, it is impossible for me to fail. My Father God is a Superstar; therefore, I am a superstar too. The world has yet to see the best of you. Paul understood this truth; that was why he declared, "I can do all things through Christ which strengtheneth me" (*Philippians 4:13*).

In a world characterized by challenges, you are bound to make a difference. The anointing of Isaac is your portion. Isaac prospered exceptionally in the midst of economic crises (*Genesis 26:1-6, 12-14*). If ever there is a time the children of God must prosper against all odds, it is now. The time of having just one stream of income is over. The Garden of Eden was watered by four streams (*Genesis 2:10*).

God wants us to prosper financially and physically to the same degree as we prosper spiritually. But He does not prosper us just for prosperity's sake; our prosperity is meant to honour Him (*Psalm 35:27*), enable us to be a blessing to others (*Genesis 12:2*), and advance His Kingdom (*Romans 10:14-15*). To reach the world with the Gospel requires huge financial resources. You must become a great Kingdom investor: bear in mind that Jesus encouraged His disciples to lay up for themselves treasures in heaven (*Matthew 6:19-21*).

When you meditate on God's Word day and night, you will be like a tree planted by rivers of water, bringing forth your fruit in your season. Your leaf shall not wither (that is, anything connected to you must thrive); and whatsoever you do shall prosper, whether the times are hard or not, and whether the devil likes it or not. It is time to speak to every area of your life and command it to prosper.

Refuse to give in to fear or discouragement! Even if you have failed in the past, get up and keep trying. Isaac never gave up; he kept on digging more wells until he came to Rehoboth (*Genesis 26:22*). Persevere until you come to your Rehoboth. Write that book; start that business; embark on that project.

Declare this as often as possible:

WHATSOEVER I DO SHALL PROSPER IN JESUS' NAME!

DAY 6—EVENING

Because I know my God, I am strong and I carry out great exploits

But the people who know their God shall be strong, and carry out great exploits.

Daniel 11:32b, NKJV

The people who know (*yada* in Hebrew; meaning "understand") their God—that is, the genuine Christians—shall be strong (*chazaq*; meaning "be constant"), strengthened by His grace and Spirit, and carry out great exploits. The impact you have in life depends not so much on *what* you know as *who* you know.

In *Hosea 4:6*, God lamented that His people were failing. Not because they were poor or unschooled or without the "right" connections, but because they lacked a proper understanding of who He was and, consequently, who they were. The greatest problem with man has always been one of identity.

To understand who God is, and how He operates, is to understand who we are, and how we are to operate. God's Word tells us that we are created in His image and likeness (*Genesis 1:26*). This means we are created to be like God and to function like God. God is Spirit; therefore, we are spirit too. We have a soul and we live in a body, but our true nature is spiritual. The offspring of a lion is a lion. If we are God's offspring, we are gods too (*Psalm 82:6*). He is The Rock of Ages; so, we are also rocks (*Deuteronomy 32:3-4*).

It is important to know that the spiritual controls the physical. Everything we see physically was first created

32

spiritually. God created the whole world by speaking it into existence *(Genesis 1:1-25).* His words carry creative power. God calls into existence those things that are not as though they are (*Romans 4:17*). We are to do likewise.

Proper knowledge of who God is—and, consequently, who we are—gives us an inner strength that renders us constant, firm and unshakable in the face of temptations and challenges. Knowledge is power. Are you feeling weak and ineffective? Check your knowledge (understanding) of God. Your ability to resist temptation is a reflection of your knowledge. Your exploits are a reflection of your strength. The greater the knowledge, the greater the strength. The greater the strength, the greater the exploits. Exploits here speak of bold, adventurous acts and brilliant achievements.

The true men and women of God left their mark on history —Abraham, Isaac, Jacob, Moses, Joshua, Gideon, David, Solomon, Daniel, Shadrach, Meshach, Abednego, Peter, Paul, and countless others. What mark are you going to leave on earth before you leave this earth? You are not a "nobody". You were born for great exploits, born to make an impact.

Remove smallness from your mind. Your God is a big God. You might start small—and, certainly, do not despise small beginnings (*Zechariah 4:10*)—but start dreaming big. Don't just write a book, but books. Don't just start a business, but businesses. Don't just get a degree, but degrees. You can do all things through Christ who strengthens you (*Philippians 4:13*).

There will always be people and circumstances that tempt us to settle for compromise and mediocrity, but we must say no to them, with all the strength derived from our knowledge of God—just as others like Daniel, Shadrach, Meshach and Abednego have done. They preferred to die rather than compromise their faith in God, for "they loved not their lives unto the death" (*Revelation 12:11*).

Jesus has assured us in *John 14:12*:

> Verily, verily, I say unto you, He that believeth on me, the works that I do shall he do also; and greater works than these shall he do; because I go unto my Father.

If you are in Christ, what are the "greater works" you have done so far? The greatest work (exploit) we can do is to preach the Gospel to those who are not yet part of God's Kingdom: get them into His Kingdom so that they can experience, enjoy and express God to the visible and invisible world. Ever since you came to Christ, how many people are in the Kingdom and enjoying the life of Christ in them, thanks to you? If you are not satisfied with what you have done so far or where you are right now in your walk with God, here is what you can do:

- Seek the face of God to understand Him better and His will for your life (*Philippians 3:10-11; Ephesians 5:17*);

- Set clear objectives as to what you want God to accomplish in and through you, now and in the future (*Proverbs 29:18; Habakkuk 2:2*);

- Perfect and discipline yourself, and seek God to endow you with His power and with all the skills and spiritual gifts needed to accomplish these objectives (*Ephesians 4:11-13; 1 Corinthians 14:1, 9:27*);

- Partner with likeminded persons (*Philippians 4:15-17; Ecclesiastes 4:9*) and train others to follow in your footsteps (*1 Corinthians 11:1; 2 Timothy 2:2*);

- Give glory to God for all your successes.

Having understood and applied what you have learnt here, you can now declare with confidence:

BECAUSE I KNOW MY GOD, I AM STRONG, AND I CARRY OUT GREAT EXPLOITS!

I am the head and not the tail

And the LORD shall make thee the head, and not the tail; and thou shalt be above only, and thou shalt not be beneath; if that thou hearken unto the commandments of the LORD thy God, which I command thee this day, to observe and to do them.

Deuteronomy 28:13

This was God's promise to the children of Israel: to make them the head and not the tail, if they obeyed Him. Because you are Abraham's seed, you are equally entitled to this promise too. As it says in *Galatians 3:29*, "And if ye be Christ's, then are ye Abraham's seed, and heirs according to the promise."

To be the head is to be at the forefront, at the top; to be excellent, to set the pace; to be the leader, ruler, chief, captain, or principal. You were not born to take second place. You were created to be first, not last; to be first class, not second class; to walk in excellence, not mediocrity. You were born into God's Kingdom to be a role model for others to follow; to be a blessing to them. So... how many people have you blessed thus far because of this top position you occupy?

The good news is that *you can do it*—not by might nor by power, but by the Spirit of God (*Zechariah 4:6*). It is the Lord who makes you the head, and He does it when you listen to Him and willingly do His will.

One thing is clear: the promises of God are not automatic. As long as you hearken unto His commandments and observe and do them, you will be the head and not the tail.

If you are a student, you will be at the top of your class and never at the bottom. If you are in business, you are going to be the market leader. If you are a professional, you will distinguish yourself in the workplace. If you are married, you will enjoy a happy, loving relationship with your spouse. In these end times, God is in the business of quickening His people, not only to stand up, but to stand out.

Why does God want to make you the head? So that you will bring glory to His name and be a blessing to others. *Proverbs 29:2* says, "When the righteous are in authority, the people rejoice: but when the wicked beareth rule, the people mourn." In these end times, God is in the business of raising men and women to be like the Josephs, Daniels, Shadrachs, Meshachs, Abednegos, Davids and Esthers of old, who will make the people rejoice so that His name might be glorified.

No matter where you are now in the scheme of things, be assured that you are bound for the top. God wants to make you the head—not to have you grow proud and selfish and dominate over people, but so that you can be a blessing to them. Can God count on you?

As for those of you who are already at the top, how are you using your privileged position to help others? And, even if you are already at the top, there are always new heights to climb. God is able to move you from glory to glory.

As it says in *2 Corinthians 3:18*:

> But we all, with open face beholding as in a glass the glory of the Lord, are changed into the same image from glory to glory, even as by the Spirit of the Lord.

As long as you are a child of God, walking in obedience to His Word, you can make this declaration with confidence:

I AM THE HEAD AND NOT THE TAIL!

I walk in freedom because I know and practise the Truth

And ye shall know the truth, and the truth shall make you free.

John 8:32

The Greek word for "know", as it is used here, is *ginosko*, which means "to be aware of" or "to understand". When you understand the truth (*aletheia*), that which is true will make you free (*eleutheroo*)—that is, it will deliver you.

What Jesus is saying here is that, when you become very familiar with, or aware of, or understand who He really is— the trustworthy One, the GENUINE ONE—you will be delivered from all falsehood about yourself, about Him, and about the world. Your life will be filled with joy, and you will become a deliverer yourself. You will begin to help others find deliverance, just like Andrew did when He met Jesus, the True One (*John 1:40-42*). No one's life remains the same after an encounter with Jesus!

Our world is filled with fake products that look like the real thing. It takes experts to distinguish the fake from the true. The truth Jesus speaks of is not something abstract but real. He speaks of Himself: "I am the way, the truth, and the life" (*John 14:6*). To know Jesus therefore is to know THE TRUTH. Not to know Jesus is to live a lie—or in lies.

The truth shall *make* you free. To "make" speaks of a process. The truth that will set us free is the truth we have hidden in our hearts and the truth that we apply. The Psalmist said in *Psalm 119:11*, "Thy word have I hid in mine heart, that I might not sin against thee."

We become what we meditate on or what we watch. We become like the persons we spend time with. Paul cautioned, "Be not deceived: evil communications corrupt good manners" (*1 Corinthians 15:33*).

The more time you spend with Jesus, listening to Him and obeying Him, the more you become like Him. The more you become like Him, the more you become a deliverer like Him. He wants to deliver us from all the falsehoods that the devil and society have imposed upon us—and from the lies that have enslaved us and stopped us from becoming all that God has called us to be. In *Matthew 4:1-11*, Jesus Himself showed us how to gain victory over the enemy. He counteracted every one of Satan's temptation with the Word of God.

Perhaps you have been brought up to see yourself as a "nobody". That is a lie. Let the Lord change that poor self-image of yours, as He did with Gideon (*Judges 6:12, 14-16*). You will then begin to see yourself as you truly are: a valued child of God, destined to carry out great exploits for Him.

The more time you spend with the TRUTH and in the TRUTH, the more you will graduate:

- from darkness to light (*Colossians 1:13*)

- from fear to boldness (*Acts 4:13, 31*)

- from stagnation to progress (*2 Corinthians 3:18*)

- from unrighteousness to righteousness (*2 Corinthians 5:21*)

- from hatred to love (*Matthew 22:36-40*)

- from mediocrity to excellence (*1 Corinthians 10:31; Genesis 1:31; Colossians 3:23*)

- from fruitlessness to fruitfulness (*John 15:16*)

- from lack to abundance (*John 10:10*)

- from poverty to prosperity (*2 Corinthians 8:9*)

- from sickness to health (*Isaiah 53:5*)

- from weakling to warrior (*Judges 6:12*)

- from failure to success (*2 Timothy 2:15; Joshua 1:8*)

No matter what you might be going through now, the answer is in the Word, and the Word is in you! Paul tells us to declare the Word with faith:

> The word is nigh thee, even in thy mouth, and in thy heart: that is, the word of faith, which we preach;
> That if thou shalt confess with thy mouth the Lord Jesus, and shalt believe in thine heart that God hath raised him from the dead, thou shalt be saved.
> For with the heart man believeth unto righteousness; and with the mouth confession is made unto salvation.
>
> *Romans 10:8-10*

In the WORD is a word for every situation we face. With this in mind, you can declare with confidence:

I WALK IN FREEDOM BECAUSE I KNOW AND PRACTISE THE TRUTH!

I am the salt of the earth and the light of the world

Ye are the salt of the earth: but if the salt have lost his savour, wherewith shall it be salted? it is thenceforth good for nothing, but to be cast out, and to be trodden under foot of men. Ye are the light of the world. A city that is set on an hill cannot be hid.

Matthew 5:13-14

Salt is used mostly for preserving or seasoning food. Salt keeps meat from going bad, from decay, and from corruption. As Christ's disciples, we are likened to salt, for we are called to preserve the world from moral corruption and hence from destruction—because whatever becomes utterly corrupted is doomed to be destroyed.

Salt is worthless if it has lost its ability to preserve food. It is then fit only to be cast out and trodden underfoot. So too with those who profess to be Christ's followers—those who are called to be the salt of the earth but who have ceased to communicate God's gospel of salvation, thereby leaving the lost to die in their moral depravity. Such "followers" are fit only to be cast out, and Christ will spew them out of His mouth (*Revelation 3:16*).

Salt also enhances the taste of food, bringing delight to those who partake of it. As children of God, our presence should bring delight everywhere we go. People should love to be around us.

We are also called to be the "light of the world"; and, as light removes darkness, so are we called to remove the darkness of ignorance, sin and sorrow. Christ has lighted us that we may enlighten the world. Paul puts it this way:

> Take no part in the worthless pleasures of evil and darkness, but instead, rebuke and expose them. It would be shameful even to mention here those pleasures of darkness that the ungodly do.
>
> But when you expose them, *the light shines in upon their sin and shows it up*, and when they see how wrong they really are, some of them may even become children of light!
>
> *Ephesians 5:11-13, TLB*

We should never hide our faith. God desires His grace to be as conspicuous as a city built on a mountain's brow. To try to conceal His Spirit is as foolish as trying to put a lamp "under a bushel": the lamp should be seen by "all who are in the house"— and so should the Christian's faith. The business of the church is not only to save but also to enlighten. Christ is light, so His disciples must be light too. Ancient cities were built on hills for the sake of defence. Such cities could be seen from afar; so too must the church shine forth its light far and wide.

As a child of God, you must realize you are indispensable for the preservation of the world from sin. Wherever you find yourself, you are there to bring joy and direction—and, without compromise, to denounce sin. Paul exhorts us:

> Do all things without murmurings and disputings: That ye may be blameless and harmless, the sons of God, without rebuke, in the midst of a crooked and perverse nation, among whom ye shine as lights in the world.
>
> *Philippians 2:14-15*

As salt and light, you can never hide your identity. Recently I was talking to a young man whose marriage had just broken down, and he said that he had always been a secret admirer of my marriage. I told him, "All marriages have their challenges." He replied that, as far as he was concerned, my marriage was worth emulating. Whether you like it or not, people are observing you every day. Are you an example for them to emulate? Paul advised Timothy:

> Let no man despise thy youth; but be thou an example of the believers, in word, in conversation, in charity, in spirit, in faith, in purity.
>
> *1 Timothy 4:12*

We are to be examples, especially to those who are not yet part of God's Kingdom. In his letter to the Colossians, Paul said:

> Servants, obey in all things your masters according to the flesh; not with eye service, as men pleasers; but in singleness of heart, fearing God; And whatsoever ye do, do it heartily, as to the Lord, and not unto men.
>
> *Colossians 3:22-23*

Actions, they say, speak louder than words. The way you treat people in your office or business speaks volumes about your God. The way you handle your time, money, position, relationships, emotions and everything else speaks volumes about your God and His Kingdom. The way you dress also matters to God. Are you seductive in your dressing? We need to watch out: everything we think, say and do matters now and in the world to come. We shall give account someday to God (*Romans 14:10; 2 Corinthians 5:10*). Let us attract more people to God's Kingdom by being worthier ambassadors for Christ (*2 Corinthians 5:20*).

Because of the presence of Christ in you (*Colossians 1:27*), you can be such a blessing to the world! You are in the world, but you are not to act like the world. You are to influence the world positively, instead of the world influencing you. Rather than hide yourself away, you must mix with people.

Salt is useful only if it is mixed with other ingredients in a dish. So too are God's children useful in His Kingdom only when they mix with people who really need them—people who are lost in sin and living tasteless lives. Jesus said He did not come for the healthy but for the sick (*Mark 2:17*). Paul also said he became all things to all men in the hope of winning some to Christ (*1 Corinthians 9:22*).

The darker the darkness, the more the need for light, and the more useful the light. There is so much darkness in the world today: wickedness, corruption, hatred, terrorism, substance abuse, occultism, religiosity, and much more. If there is ever a time the world needs God's children to shine their light into its darkness, the time is now (*Romans 8:19; Isaiah 60:1-2*).

The time is now, and the rewards are for all eternity:

And they that be wise shall shine as the brightness of the firmament; and they that turn many to righteousness as the stars for ever and ever.

Daniel 12:3

No matter how challenging it might be to live in this crooked world, you must truthfully confess that:

**I AM THE SALT OF THE EARTH AND
THE LIGHT OF THE WORLD!**

Because I have the revelation of Jesus, I am blessed

Simon Peter answered and said, Thou art the Christ, the Son of the living God. Jesus answered and said unto him, Blessed art thou, Simon Barjona: for flesh and blood hath not revealed it unto thee, but my Father which is in heaven.

Matthew 16:16-17

Peter received the revelation that Jesus is the Christ, the Son of the living God. Whoever has that revelation is supremely blessed—which, by extension, means that he or she is privileged, fortunate, well-off, prosperous and happy.

"Christ" comes from the Greek word *Christos*, meaning "the Anointed One". It is the equivalent of the Hebrew *Mashiach* (from which we get "Messiah"), meaning "the Consecrated or Anointed One". This title is given preeminently to our Lord and Saviour. "Son of the living God" means "manifestation of the living God" or "the God-Man". We will explore these terms further, to appreciate why Jesus said that Peter was so blessed.

Having been instructed by their prophets, the ancient Jews had a clear and true concept of the Messiah. But their expectations gradually became so depraved that, by the time Jesus appeared in Judea, the people were entertaining totally different and false notions of the Messiah. They expected a temporal monarch and conqueror who would remove the Roman yoke from the Jews and rule over the whole world.

Hence, they were scandalized by the outward appearance of our Saviour—His humility and seeming weakness. The modern Jews have made even greater mistakes, forming for themselves ideas of the Messiah utterly unknown to their forefathers.

The ancient prophets had foretold that the Messiah would be both God and man; Master and Servant; Priest and victim; Prince and subject; rich, yet poor; exalted, yet abased; victim of death, yet victor over death; a glorious King and Conqueror, yet a Man of grief, exposed to infirmities, in a state of abjection and humiliation. All these contrarieties were to be reconciled in the person of the Messiah—as they really were in the Person of Jesus.

It is not recorded that Christ ever received any external official unction. The unction that He did receive, which the prophets and apostles spoke of, was the spiritual and internal unction of grace and of the Holy Spirit. The official unction with which kings, priests and prophets were anointed in ancient times was but a figure and symbol of this internal spiritual unction of the Holy Spirit.

The name CHRIST is the official title of the Redeemer. It is not to be regarded as a mere appellative to distinguish our Lord from other persons named Jesus. If we overlook the significance of this name, we will miss the full impact of many passages of Scripture.

We may get the true sense of such passages by substituting, in place of the word "Christ," the title "The Anointed"; or, where Jews are addressed, "The Messiah". For example, *Matthew 2:4* tells us that King Herod demanded to know "where Christ should be born". If we were to change this to Herod demanding to know "where *the Messiah* should be born", we will begin to get the full force of what this news meant to the king.

Similarly, in *Matthew 16:16*, when Peter said to Jesus, "Thou art the Christ", what he was actually saying was, "Thou art *the Messiah.*" In *Luke 4:41*, the devils did the same. In later times, the name Jesus was used less frequently and "Christ", as a proper name, was used more often than "Jesus" to refer to our Lord.

When we consider how Christ, who was God, yet became a man; when we consider His work as our Prophet, Priest and King; when we consider how He divested Himself of all His glory to suffer the humiliation of the cross; and when we consider how all the perfections of God are displayed and all the truths of God exemplified in Him, we have a delightful view of Him as ALL and IN ALL (*Colossians 3:11*).

Paul considered it a mystery that Christ, being God, became a man:

> And without controversy great is the mystery of godliness: God was manifest in the flesh, justified in the Spirit, seen of angels, preached unto the Gentiles, believed on in the world, received up into glory.
>
> *1 Timothy 3:16*

This is a mystery to us because our finite human minds cannot comprehend how ALMIGHTY GOD could have condescended to come and live inside a human being. But what is impossible with man is possible with God.

God in His original nature is Spirit (*John 4:23-24*). As Spirit, He could not save man. To save man, God needed to have a physical body, so that He could shed His blood for man's sins—for "without shedding of blood" there is "no remission" of sins (*Hebrews 9:22*). Peter acknowledged that Jesus was "Christ, the Son of the living God" (*Matthew 16:16*). The word "Son" is used here in the sense of Jesus being considered a "vessel", "temple" or "image" of the living God.

In the Old Testament, God assumed various forms to accomplish His purposes. He led the children of Israel in a pillar of cloud and of fire (*Exodus 13:21*). He embodied the rock that released water for the Israelites in the wilderness (*Numbers 20:8; 1 Corinthians 10:4*). He revealed Himself to Abraham as a man (*Genesis 18:1-5*) and also as a priest (*Genesis 14:18; Hebrews 7:1-3*).

This explains why all of us who have received Christ are also called sons and daughters of God or the "temple" of God (*John 1:12; 1 Corinthians 6:19-20*). We are blessed in every way because our sins are forgiven and we are at peace with ***the Almighty, who is living in us to direct our steps.***

You are blessed when you come to the understanding that the God of the universe dwells in you: "Christ in you, the hope of glory" (*Colossians 1:27*). You have the seven Spirits of God in you: the Spirit of the LORD; the Spirit of wisdom and of understanding; the Spirit of counsel and of might; the Spirit of knowledge and of the fear of God (*Isaiah 11:1-2*). How can you fail when you are so filled with God's Spirit? You are not only blessed, but you are blessed to be a blessing. You are blessed to help reconcile people to God, so that they can enjoy having His Spirit in them too.

With this understanding, you can now declare with confidence:

BECAUSE I HAVE THE REVELATION OF JESUS, I AM BLESSED!

I am a god: I think like one, I talk like one, and I act like one

I have said, Ye are gods; and all of you are children of the most High.

Psalm 82:6

That which is born of the flesh is flesh; and that which is born of the Spirit is spirit.

John 3:6

For most of God's children, life has been too "natural" to a fault. By this, I mean that we live our lives too much in the natural (physical) realm. But God is a Spirit (*John 4:24*), so it is high time we started walking like the spiritual, supernatural beings that we are—if indeed we have been recreated in Christ.

If a lion cub were to grow up among a flock of sheep, it would be very easy for it to start feeling and acting like one of them. But, at heart, a lion is still a lion for as long as it lives. To be God's child is to be His offspring: it is to take after God, to be like Him. It is to be His representative on earth.

To be God's children is to be mighty. God stands in the congregation of the mighty and makes an assessment of what His offspring are up to (*Psalm 82:1*). They are supposed to judge justly. They are to defend the poor and the fatherless. They are to do justice to the afflicted and needy. They are to deliver the poor and needy out of the hand of the wicked. But God laments that His offspring are ignorant of who they are and whose they are (*Psalm 82:3-5*).

In *Hosea 4:6*, we see this same problem occurring again among God's people. God says of them:

My people are destroyed for lack of knowledge: because thou hast rejected knowledge, I will also reject thee, that thou shalt be no priest to me: seeing thou hast forgotten the law of thy God, I will also forget thy children.

God's children did not understand what was expected of them or how they could make a difference in the world. Because of their ignorance and lack of understanding, they walked on in darkness and ended up falling and dying (*Psalm 82:7*). But this shall not be your portion, in Jesus' name!

How can you make a difference in these end times? All you need to do is to follow in the footsteps of Jesus. The people of Jesus' day were scandalized when He called God His Father and told them He was the Son of God—or, worse still, one with God (*John 10:30-39*). They were scandalized because the natural man does not understand the things of God, which can only be spiritually discerned (*1 Corinthians 2:14*).

However, if you are born of the Spirit of God, you are a god. Lions give birth to lions; elephants give birth to elephants; and, therefore, God gives birth to gods. Jesus is an example of what gods are supposed to be:

God anointed Jesus of Nazareth with the Holy Ghost and with power: **who went about doing good, and healing all** that were oppressed of the devil; for God was with him.

Acts 10:38

Gods do not dominate their fellow human beings, but they make life easier for the oppressed and downtrodden. As a god, you are to seek God's anointing and power so that you can follow in Jesus' steps and do even more than He did; for He Himself has assured us that we are able to do it:

> Verily, verily, I say unto you, He that believeth on me, the works that I do shall he do also; and greater works than these shall he do; because I go unto my Father.
>
> *John 14:12*

Jesus is the King of kings. He is your King, and you are a king under Him. Now, as a king, your words have power:

> Where the word of a king is, there is power: and who may say unto him, What doest thou?
>
> *Ecclesiastes 8:4*

What matters is what God says of His children and not what others say of them or what His children think of themselves. God says we are gods. It does not matter what others say of us or what we think of ourselves. You don't need to feel like a god to be a god. As long as you are born of the Spirit of God, just declare this with confidence and see your life turn around for the better:

I AM A GOD: I THINK LIKE ONE, I TALK LIKE ONE, AND I ACT LIKE ONE, IN THE NAME OF JESUS!

The Lord is my Shepherd, I shall not be in want

The LORD is my shepherd; I shall not want.

Psalm 23:1

Of all the verses in the Bible, this happens to be one of the most popular. The word "shepherd" comes from the Hebrew word *ra'ah*, which means "to tend a flock"—that is, "to pasture" it; to be a herdsman or **keeper** (of sheep); or, by extension, to be a pastor. Generally, it means "to rule"; or, by extension, to "associate with" or "make friends with", or to "keep company with" someone (as a **friend** or **companion**).

The word "want" is from the Hebrew word *chaser*, which means "to lack"—by implication, "to fail", "to lessen", "to decrease", "to be abated", or "to be bereaved".

When we put these two words— "shepherd" and "want" — together, it becomes clear to us that the Psalmist David was making a powerful assertion of who God was to him. *Psalm 23* speaks of the intimacy David had with God. The relationship between God and him was as intimate as the close relationship he had as a shepherd boy with his sheep. Therefore, David could confidently say, "Because God is my friend, I can never lack any good thing. I can never decrease or fail or be made lower or be put to shame."

In short, David was saying, "God is my sufficiency." Why did he say this? Because he had come to know this truth about God: that He is not only a Shepherd, but a *good* one.

51

While tending his father's sheep, David had experienced God's care and protection. God took care of his needs and preserved him from the wild animals. By the grace of God, this young boy was able to kill lions and bears with his bare hands!

David knew God as his Creator. And, because he was God's property, he could never be abandoned by the God he knew to be caring, sacrificial and protective. As Jesus said:

> I am the good shepherd: the good shepherd giveth his life for the sheep. But he that is an hireling, and not the shepherd, whose own the sheep are not, seeth the wolf coming, and leaveth the sheep, and fleeth: and the wolf catcheth them, and scattereth the sheep.
>
> *John 10:11-12*

David's knowledge of God was not merely intellectual: he had experienced the goodness and greatness of God. Jesus said in *John 10:14*, "I am the good shepherd, and know my sheep, and am known of mine." When we study the rest of *Psalm 23*, we will have a better understanding of what it means for God to be our Good Shepherd. To begin with, He is our source of provision for every physical need:

> He maketh me to lie down in green pastures: he leadeth me beside the still waters.
>
> *Psalm 23:2*

He is also our source of emotional and spiritual satisfaction:

> He restoreth my soul: he leadeth me in the paths of righteousness for his name's sake.
>
> *Psalm 23:3*

He is our source of protection too:

Yea, though I walk through the valley of the shadow of death, I will fear no evil: for thou art with me...

Psalm 23:4

He is also our source of prosperity, promoting and uplifting us:

> Thou preparest a table before me in the presence of mine enemies: thou anointest my head with oil; my cup runneth over.
>
> *Psalm 23:5*

In summary, God is our source of TOTAL satisfaction—physical, emotional, spiritual and social:

> Surely goodness and mercy shall follow me all the days of my life: and I will dwell in the house of the Lord for ever.
>
> *Psalm 23:6*

God is dependable. People may let us down, but God never fails those who trust in Him and know Him as their friend. Is Jesus your friend? How deep is your knowledge of Him? Seek to know Him for yourself. Do not depend on what others say about Him. He has promised that, when we seek Him with all our hearts, we will find Him (*Jeremiah 29:11-13*).

Do you know God the way David knew God? God said of David that he was a man after His own heart (*1 Samuel 13:14*). This is not to say that David was faultless, but his secret lay in his eagerness to confess his faults before God and to please Him (*Psalm 51*). Paul was another man who deeply desired to know Christ intimately (*Philippians 3:10-11*). Tell God you want to know Him as David and Paul did... and even more!

David did not say, "The Lord is *our* Shepherd and *we* shall not want." He personalized it: "*My* Shepherd"; "*I* shall not want". The truth is, God *is* our Shepherd and we shall not want, but He wants a personal relationship with each one of us. The more intimate you become with Jesus, the more you will see results like David did, as you declare with confidence:

THE LORD IS MY SHEPHERD,
I SHALL NOT BE IN WANT!

I am a new creation: the old has gone, all things have become new

Therefore if any man be in Christ, he is a new creature: old things are passed away; behold, all things are become new.

2 Corinthians 5:17

To be "in Christ" is to be united with Him through faith. When you are united with Christ, you become a new creation: God has put away the old and brought in the new. You are not a reformation or a remolding of your former self. You are a new creature, an original production, a special species that did not exist before: "that ye put on the new man, which after God is created in righteousness and true holiness" (*Ephesians 4:24*).

"Old things are passed away" implies that previously-held views and beliefs about spiritual things are changed. "Become new" means that one seeks new ends, pursues a new course of conduct, and has new joys and new sorrows, new hopes and new fears, new relationships and new prospects.

And have put on the new man, which is renewed in knowledge after the image of him that created him.

Colossians 3:10

For we are... created *in Christ Jesus* unto good works which God hath before ordained that we should walk in them.

Ephesians 2:10

54

Jesus' words and ways were too new and radical for the men of His day to handle. He commented about them:

> Neither do men put new wine into old bottles: else the bottles break, and the wine runneth out, and the bottles perish: but they put new wine into new bottles, and both are preserved.
>
> *Matthew 9:17*

No doubt your former associates will also be disgusted with the new person you have become (*1 Peter 4:4*), but do not be discouraged by this; just let your life be a testimony to them.

It is not possible to be in Christ or to be one with the Spirit of Christ and not love the things that Christ loves and hate the things that Christ hates. Certainly, true Christianity is not about rules and regulations. But how can I be in Christ, and still love the same sinful places and pleasures I used to love? How can I continue to dance to the same kind of ungodly music as before? My body is now the temple of the Holy Spirit (*1 Corinthians 3:16*); I can't use it for immoral purposes. I can't continue to live the same kind of worldly lifestyle I used to live before. The Bible is clear about this:

> Love not the world, neither the things that are in the world. If any man love the world, the love of the Father is not in him.
>
> For all that is in the world, the lust of the flesh, and the lust of the eyes, and the pride of life, is not of the Father, but is of the world.
>
> And the world passeth away, and the lust thereof: but he that doeth the will of God abideth for ever.
>
> *1 John 2:15-17*

John the Baptist told his listeners to prove their repentance by their fruit (*Matthew 3:8-10*). Jesus has also said, "Ye shall know them by their fruits" (*Matthew 7:16*). Zacchaeus is a good example of a new creation in Christ, who proved his repentance by his fruit:

> And Zacchaeus stood, and said unto the Lord: Behold, Lord, the half of my goods I give to the poor; and if I have taken anything from any man by false accusation, I restore him fourfold.
>
> And Jesus said unto him, This day is salvation come to this house, forsomuch as he also is a son of Abraham.
>
> *Luke 19:8-9*

Certainly, some changes will be dramatic while others will take more time. But one thing is certain: when Christ truly takes over, you *will* change direction. While Paul's change was dramatic (*Acts 9:1-20*), Peter's was gradual (*Luke 22:31-32*); but both exemplified Christlikeness.

If man's spiritual condition bothered Christ, it should also bother you (*Matthew 9:35-37*). If He stooped to wash the disciples' feet (*John 13:1-17*), so must you be ready to stoop low to glorify Him. You are now His hands, His feet, His mouth, His eyes, His ears, and His Body. It has been given to you not only to believe in Christ, but also to suffer for Him (*Philippians 1:29*); to obey His command to love as He has loved you:

> By this shall all men know that ye are my disciples, if ye have love one to another.
>
> *John 13:35*

As you go through life with all its challenges, resist the temptation to compromise. Confess that:

**I AM A NEW CREATION; THE OLD HAS GONE,
ALL THINGS HAVE BECOME NEW!**

The Lord is my great Light, I shall not walk in the dark

The people that walked in darkness have seen a great light: they that dwell in the land of the shadow of death, upon them hath the light shined.

Isaiah 9:2

This prophecy by Isaiah foretold the coming of Jesus, proclaiming Him to be not only the light of the world but a GREAT LIGHT. The greatness of this light was made manifest to the people who dwelt in the dark and in the shadow of death. This refers to the land of Zebulun, Naphtali and Manasseh—that is, the country of Galilee all around the sea of Gennesaret.

These areas suffered the most in the first Assyrian invasion under Tiglath-Pileser (*2 Kings 15:29; 1 Chronicles 5:26*). They were also the first to enjoy the blessings of Christ's ministry as He preached the Gospel and performed miracles among them. God delights in revealing Himself to the dejected, rejected, despised and depressed; as it says in *1 Corinthians 1:26-31*:

> For ye see your calling, brethren, how that not many wise men after the flesh, not many mighty, not many noble, are called: But God hath chosen the foolish things of the world to confound the wise; and... the weak things of the world to confound the things which are mighty;
>
> And base things of the world, and things which are despised, hath God chosen, yea, and things which are not, to bring to nought things that are:

That no flesh should glory in his presence. But of him are ye in Christ Jesus, who of God is made unto us wisdom, and righteousness, and sanctification, and redemption: That, according as it is written, He that glorieth, let him glory in the Lord.

The greater the darkness you are going through, the greater will the light of Christ shine on you—if you give Him the opportunity. Jesus came to His own, but His own did not receive Him. But as many as receive Him, as many as believe in Him, to them He gives the right to become the children of God and to experience His power in their lives (*John 1:11-13*).

Are you going through any form of thick darkness in your life? The thick darkness of sin or sickness or shortage or shyness or satanic oppression? No darkness can be stronger than the Light of Christ. When the light appears, darkness has no choice but to disappear. The Bible says that God is Light and in Him there is no darkness at all (*1 John 1:5*).

Darkness speaks of all that is negative. Sad to say that, though the Light has come into the world, men prefer the darkness because their deeds are evil (*John 3:19*).

To belong to Christ is to walk in the light: "if we walk in the light, as he is in the light... the blood of Jesus Christ... cleanseth us from all sin" (*1 John 1:7*). The greatness of Christ's light speaks of salvation, healing, deliverance and blessings. His greatness is available to all who trust in Him:

But without faith it is impossible to please him: for he that cometh to God must believe that he is, and that he is a rewarder of them that diligently seek him.

Hebrews 11:6

For whatsoever is born of God overcometh the world: and this is the victory that overcometh the world, even our faith.

1 John 5:4

Are you already experiencing the power of Christ in your life? If yes, praise God. You can go from glory to glory, by the Spirit of the Lord (*2 Corinthians 3:18*). If you have yet to experience this great power, you can do so by asking Jesus to come into your heart and take control of your life (*Romans 10:9-10*).

The enemy wants you to focus on the greatness of your problems instead of the greatness of Jesus. But do not fall into his trap; do not be intimidated by him. Fix your eyes on Jesus; declare as the Psalmist did:

> The LORD is my light and my salvation; whom shall I fear? The LORD is the strength of my life; of whom shall I be afraid?
>
> *Psalm 27:1*

The more you focus on the greatness of Jesus, the lesser your problems become, and the more you can experience His power at work in your life. Blind Bartimaeus was one man who displayed an impressive faith. He was so bent on experiencing the awesome power of Jesus that, the more his fellowmen put barriers in his way, the more he refused to give in to them:

> And many charged him that he should hold his peace: but he cried the more a great deal, Thou son of David, have mercy on me.
>
> *Mark 10:48*

Jesus heard his cry and restored his sight. He can do the same for you, and even greater miracles than that! Simply declare with confidence:

**THE LORD IS MY GREAT LIGHT,
I SHALL NOT WALK IN THE DARK!**

I am blessed in my coming in and my going out

Blessed shalt thou be when thou comest in, and blessed shalt thou be when thou goest out.

Deuteronomy 28:6

God's desire for His children is all-round blessings. To be blessed in your coming in is to be blessed in your family life. You shall have peace with your spouse (if you are married), your children (if you are a parent), your parents and your siblings. There shall be love and understanding in your home, and you will enjoy the company of your family members.

The husband will love the wife as Christ loved the church and gave Himself for her, and the wife will be submissive to her husband as to the Lord. The children shall be obedient to their parents and honor them, while the parents will take good care of their children and bring them up in the fear of the Lord (*Ephesians 5:22-6:1-4*).

If you are a married man, your wife shall be "like a fruitful vine *in the very heart of your house*" (*Psalm 128:3a, NKJV*). What this means is that she will be a faithful and fruitful wife—unlike the faithless wife who was "loud and rebellious, her feet would not stay at home" (*Proverbs 7:11, NKJV*).

Your children will be "like olive plants around about thy table" (*Psalm 128:3b*). Like the olive plants that symbolize productivity, your kids will do well in school and in all their endeavors. And each family meal will be a joyful occasion.

If you are a woman, you will be loved and appreciated by your family. *Proverbs 31:28* says that "Her children arise up, and call her blessed; her husband also, and he praiseth her."

A happy home is the springboard to fulfillment in life. God created the home to be heaven on earth. A healthy home gives birth to a healthy society. Do not let the devil sow seeds of discord, pain and confusion in your home. God's blessing is not automatic; play your role as God grants you grace, and He will take care of the rest.

To be blessed when you go out is to be blessed in your enterprises. God has ordained you to be successful in your work and your business endeavors. Whatever you do outside of the home will be successful. The Lord is with you, to give you the wisdom and strength you need to carry out your work and your business. In *Deuteronomy 8:18*, God says:

> But thou shalt remember the Lord thy God: for it is he that giveth thee power to get wealth, that he may establish his covenant which he sware unto thy fathers, as it is this day.

Step out with confidence, knowing that you can't fail, no matter what the challenges are. If you are working for an enterprise, it is a privilege for them to have you. You will be excellent, exemplary, hardworking, disciplined and obedient. As you perform your duties well, promotion will be your portion, in the name of Jesus! If you are running your own business, you will be at the cutting edge. Your goods and services will be the best in the market.

No matter how bleak the situation looks right now, always remember that you are blessed in and out of your home. Declare audaciously in the devil's hearing that:

I AM BLESSED IN MY COMING IN AND MY GOING OUT, IN JESUS' NAME!

Because I am connected to Christ, I am from above and above all

He that cometh from above is above all: he that is of the earth is earthly, and speaketh of the earth: he that cometh from heaven is above all.

John 3:31

Man's greatest problem has always been one of identity. *Genesis 1:26* tells us that man was created in the image and likeness of God. What this means is that he was created to be and to function like his Creator: he was created to be like God, righteous and holy (*Ephesians 4:24*) and to be able, like God, to call those things which do not exist as though they did (*Romans 4:17, NKJV*).

In *Hosea 4:6*, God said, "My people are destroyed for lack of knowledge." Because Eve was ignorant of her godlike identity, she was easily deceived by the devil. He told her that, if she ate the forbidden fruit, she was going to be like God (*Genesis 3:5*).

In fact, since she was made in God's image and likeness, she was *already* like God; but she did not know that. As a result of Adam and Eve's fall, sin came and tarnished God's image and likeness in man. But we give thanks to Christ, who has restored His image and likeness in us.

The story is told of an eaglet that was separated from its mother. It grew up among chickens and quickly adopted their ways. But, as time went on, it began to sense it was born for greater things than to live out its life as a chicken. This feeling intensified as the eaglet grew into young adulthood.

One day, the mother eagle happened to be flying over the chickens and it spotted the now-grownup eagle, still living among the chickens. It called out to its offspring on the ground to come up high, for its place was not with the chickens. The young eagle heeded the call of its mother. At once it left the chickens and flew up into the sky to join the class of eagles, to which it rightfully belonged.

If you are born of the Spirit of God, you belong to the class of God. You are an eagle, not a chicken. You might have spent all your life among chickens—to the point that you have developed a chicken mentality, and you see yourself as a chicken, and you talk like a chicken, and you go about scratching in the ground for food like a chicken. Other chickens call you "chicken" and indeed you have lost all your confidence, all because you lack knowledge about your true identity. But, in spite of all that your circumstances and the people around you might be saying, you are *not* a chicken.

Gideon had a chicken mentality until the day God appeared to him and called him, "you mighty man of valor!" (*Judges 6:12*). What matters is not what you say of yourself or what others say about you, but what God says about you.

If you are born of God, you are a god (*Psalm 82:6*). You are from above and you are above all. Your citizenship is in heaven and not on earth. You are a citizen of God's Kingdom:

> For our citizenship is in heaven, from which we also eagerly wait for the Savior, the Lord Jesus Christ.
>
> *Philippians 3:20, NKJV*

That which is from above is above all. And whatever is born of God overcomes the world (*1 John 5:4*). Because you are from above and above all, you must always think like someone from above: someone who is seated with Christ in heavenly places, far above principalities and powers.

> [God] raised us up together, and made us sit together in the heavenly places in Christ Jesus.
>
> *Ephesians 2:6, NKJV*

Satan, sickness, poverty, lack, confusion, failure, stagnation, fruitlessness and all other negative things are under your feet. You are above all that is negative or earthly.

We live on earth, but we are not of the earth. Difficulties, setbacks, challenges and even spiritual attacks might at times cause us to lapse in our faith; but they are all opportunities for the power and nature of God that is in us to be made manifest. And we thank God for His apostles, prophets, evangelists, pastors and teachers, who help us grow to maturity in Christ, so that we can begin to function as we were meant to function (*Ephesians 4:11-16*).

Jesus succeeded in His mission on earth because He knew who He was, where He came from, and where He was going. He knew how to blend His divinity with His humanity. He was fully divine, yet humble; fully human, yet sinless. We too can think, talk and act like Him. Like Father, like child. A lion can only give birth to a lion cub and not a chicken. God therefore can only give birth to gods. If I hail from God, then I must be like God and act like God. Bearing this in mind, you can declare with all confidence:

BECAUSE I AM CONNECTED TO CHRIST,
I AM FROM ABOVE AND ABOVE ALL!

My body is the temple of God, I honor God with my body

Do you not know that you are the temple of God and that the Spirit of God dwells in you?

1 Corinthians 3:16, NKJV

The word used here for "temple" comes from the Greek *naos*, which means the inner chamber or sanctuary of a temple: that is, the habitation or dwelling place or house of God. The house of God is holy. It is clean. It is pure. It is consecrated. It is sacred. Because I carry God within me, my life must be clean. Paul considered this to be a matter of such importance that he emphasized it more than once in his exhortations:

> I beseech you therefore, brethren, by the mercies of God, that ye present your bodies a living sacrifice, holy, acceptable unto God, which is your reasonable service. And be not conformed to this world: but be ye transformed by the renewing of your mind, that ye may prove what is that good, and acceptable, and perfect will of God.
>
> *Romans 12:1-2*

What? Know ye not that your body is the temple of the Holy Ghost which is in you, which ye have of God, and ye are not your own?

For ye are bought with a price: therefore glorify God in your body, and in your spirit, which are God's.

1 Corinthians 6:19-20

My body is not my own; I have been bought with the precious blood of Jesus. I must honor God with my body. My mouth must honor God; I must watch the words coming out of it. I must make sure that my words are building and not destroying my fellow human beings, who have been created in God's image. I must be careful what my eyes are watching, for it has the capacity to build me or corrupt me. Pornography is not for me.

My thoughts too must glorify God. God says that to look at a woman or man lustfully is to commit adultery in my heart (*Matthew 5:28*). I must watch my heart above all else, for out of it come the issues of life. As a man thinks in his heart, so is he (*Proverbs 4:23, 23:7*).

I must watch what I do with my body. It is not for sexual immorality or alcoholism or other forms of unrighteousness:

> Know ye not that the unrighteous shall not inherit the kingdom of God? Be not deceived: neither fornicators, nor idolaters, nor adulterers, nor effeminate, nor abusers of themselves with mankind, nor thieves, nor covetous, nor drunkards, nor revilers, nor extortioners, shall inherit the kingdom of God.
>
> *1 Corinthians 6:9-10*

> Wine is a mocker, strong drink is raging: and whosoever is deceived thereby is not wise.
>
> *Proverbs 20:1*

My mouth is not for telling lies. My hands are not for stealing. My feet are not to be taken to wrong places; they should carry me to preach the Gospel of God's Kingdom. My body is not to be used for dancing to ungodly music, or smoking cigarettes, or taking destructive drugs. In a polluted world, I am called to make a difference and to constantly confess:

MY BODY IS THE TEMPLE OF GOD, I HONOR GOD WITH MY BODY!

I believe in God and I am established; I believe His prophets and I prosper

Believe in the LORD your God, so shall ye be established; believe his prophets, so shall ye prosper.

2 Chronicles 20:20b

If we want God to prosper us, we need to follow the principles (laws) of His Kingdom. The first principle is to be established (that is, grounded) in Him, in His Word, and in the knowledge of His will. We do this by trusting in His Word, which means meditating on it and doing what it says (*Joshua 1:8*).

Secondly, to prosper in what God has called us to do, we need the ministry of His prophets. Prophets are not only those who predict the future; they can be our Pastors or people who hear from God and bring us special messages from Him. Their prophecies should accord with what God has already said in His Word—which means we need to be grounded in the Bible, so that we will not be led astray by those who call themselves prophets but do not speak in conformity with God's Word.

We live in an instant age where people want quick results. It is a fast-paced world. Many, because they are not grounded in Scripture, are easily deceived by self-styled prophets. How much time do you spend studying the Bible? Jesus told Martha "only one thing matters" (*Luke 10:42, TV*); that one thing is God's Word, which Mary had chosen. God commends and blesses those who, like Mary, hunger and thirst after His Word (righteousness), and He promises that they shall be filled (*Matthew 5:6*). When Jesus was tempted by Satan, He declared, "Man shall not live by bread alone, but by every word that comes out of the mouth of God" (*Matthew 4:4, AMP*).

The Berean Christians were said to be of a more noble character because they searched the Scriptures daily to see if what they were taught was accurate (*Acts 17:11*). Time invested in studying God's Word can never be time wasted. *Psalm 119:130* tells us, "The entrance of thy words giveth light; it giveth understanding unto the simple."

There is a word of God for us concerning every area of our lives. When we study the Bible prayerfully with the help of the Holy Spirit, we become established in the things of God. We will not be easily deceived by anyone, because we will know the mind of God concerning all that matters in life:

- Faith
- Family
- Friends
- Fitness
- Finances
- Firm (or business)
- Future

In line with the foregoing, Paul exhorts us, "Study to shew thyself approved unto God, a workman that needeth not to be ashamed, rightly dividing the word of truth" (*2 Timothy 2:15*).

To believe requires knowledge. The dictionary defines belief as being sure (that is, having the knowledge) of the truth of something; being sure (knowing) that someone is telling us the truth. To believe in someone is to be of the opinion that he or she is trustworthy. The children of Israel failed to possess the Promised Land because, though they heard God's word, they did not believe Him (*Hebrews 4:2*).

When you believe God will never leave you nor forsake you, you will stand firm in the midst of trials. Even if everyone abandons you, you will not become depressed—because you believe God is with you. You will be stable, because you are established by God's Word. This was David's secret when the enemy stole his family and property in his days of trial; he encouraged himself in the Lord, because he had been established by the Word of God (*1 Samuel 30:6; Psalm 27:13*).

How you respond in the midst of trials depends on your intake of God's Word. *It is one thing to have God's Word in you, and another thing for God to have you through His Word. To believe God is to let God's Word have you.* When this is done, then the ministry of God's prophet will open the door to your prosperity.

To believe God's prophet is to act according to the instructions God has given through His prophet. This was what the widow in *2 Kings 4:1-7* did, when she was about to lose her sons to her late husband's creditor; she acted according to the Prophet Elisha's instructions, and her problem was solved and she prospered.

When a vast army came to wage war against King Jehoshaphat and the children of Israel, it would have been very easy for them to panic. But, instead, they called upon the God they believed in, and He answered them through His Prophet Jahaziel, who assured them, "Do not be afraid... for the battle is not yours, but God's" (*2 Chronicles 20:15*).

Jehoshaphat and the people believed God, and they were established in confidence. They obeyed God's prophet when he told them, "Do not fear or be dismayed; tomorrow go out against them, for the LORD is with you" (*2 Chronicles 20:17*). They obeyed the prophetic word of God, and He gave them one of the greatest victories Israel has ever had. God fought for them, for the battle was His (*2 Chronicles 20:20-29*).

When we are faced with challenging situations, it is easy to panic and forget God's promises, which are meant to establish us. But, instead of panicking, learn to run to God, like Jehoshaphat and the children of Israel did. Remember God's promises, and your faith in Him will be strengthened. Ask Him to give you a word about the situation before you. Fear is not of God. The spirit God has given us is one of boldness, of a sound mind, and of self-control (*2 Timothy 1:7*).

Perhaps you have received a bad report from the doctor, or you are faced with unpaid bills, or your child is on drugs, or your marriage is not working out, or your business is failing. Whatever your problem, there is a word of God for you. When poverty strikes, tell yourself that God has promised to supply all your needs according to His riches in glory, as you faithfully sow into His Kingdom (*Philippians 4:19; Luke 6:38*). When you fall sick, affirm that God is your Healer (*Exodus 15:26*). When you are feeling discouraged or lonely, remember that God will never leave you nor forsake you (*Hebrews 13:5*).

Perhaps you have fallen into sin and are feeling condemned. Ask God for forgiveness. If you have offended anyone, seek for forgiveness and receive it by faith. You are the righteousness of God (*2 Corinthians 5:21*); there is now no condemnation for those who are in Christ Jesus, who walk not after the flesh but after the Spirit (*Romans 8:1*).

Your destiny is in God's hands; to despise Him or His prophets is to opt for defeat. How is your relationship with God, and who is He presently using to speak into your life? To be established in the things of God and to prosper in life, it is crucial to have the kind of faith that Joshua and Caleb did (*Numbers 14:6-9*). To build your faith, declare confidently:

**I BELIEVE IN GOD AND I AM ESTABLISHED,
I BELIEVE HIS PROPHETS AND I PROSPER!**

No weapon formed against me shall prosper

No weapon that is formed against thee shall prosper...

Isaiah 54:17(a)

Because I am a child of God, anything that has been devised against me shall certainly fail. The enemy is always working to bring down God's people. The enemy's weapons will be formed, but those weapons will not succeed in bringing me down. The One in me and with me is greater than any means of destruction that man or the forces of darkness can invent. This is in line with what Jesus said:

> And I say also unto thee, That thou art Peter, and upon this rock I will build my church; and the gates of hell shall not prevail against it.
>
> *Matthew 16:18*

You can count on God's protection. No room for panic. Fear is not of God. God has not given you a spirit of fear or of timidity (*2 Timothy 1:7*). Whenever the enemy tries to intimidate you, remember God's promises to you:

> Behold, they shall surely gather together, but not by me: whosoever shall gather together against thee shall fall for thy sake.
>
> *Isaiah 54:15*

He suffered no man to do them wrong: yea, he reproved kings for their sakes; Saying, Touch not mine anointed, and do my prophets no harm.

Psalm 105:14-15

And I give unto them eternal life; and they shall never perish, neither shall any man pluck them out of my hand.

My Father, which gave them me, is greater than all; and no man is able to pluck them out of my Father's hand.

John 10:28-29

There is therefore now no condemnation to them which are in Christ Jesus, who walk not after the flesh, but after the Spirit.

Romans 8:1

No matter what instrument of harm the enemy is trying to use against you, it shall not work. His weapons will fail him, but yours will never fail. Go on the offensive. For the Word of God that comes out of your mouth is as a "fire" that consumes your opponents and as a "hammer" that breaks their sin-hardened hearts into pieces (*Jeremiah 23:29*).

You are covered by the Almighty, like a chick that is covered by its mother hen. As the Psalmist puts it:

He that dwelleth in the secret place of the most High shall abide under the shadow of the Almighty.

Psalm 91:1

Every curse formed against you shall fail, because whatever God has blessed cannot be cursed. You are blessed of God, like the children of Israel, and therefore you cannot be cursed (*Numbers 22:12*).

So, declare throughout this day with confidence:

NO WEAPON FORMED AGAINST ME SHALL PROSPER!

Because I am discipled in Christ, I am a disciple maker

"Go therefore and make disciples of all the nations, baptizing them in the name of the Father and of the Son and of the Holy Spirit, teaching them to observe all things that I have commanded you; and lo, I am with you always, even to the end of the age." Amen.

Matthew 28:19-20, NKJV

A disciple is a student (*mathetes* in Greek) or apprentice. When we receive Christ, we become His students. Jesus was not impressed by multitudes following after Him. He was keener to make disciples, and He gave His disciples the commission to help others become His students too. The destiny of nations depends on our taking discipleship in Christ seriously. It is only when we are true disciples of Christ that we can effectively accomplish the purpose for which we have been created:

> But ye are a chosen generation, a royal priesthood, an holy nation, a peculiar people; that ye should shew forth the praises of him who hath called you out of darkness into his marvellous light.
>
> *1 Peter 2:9*

What does it take to be a disciple of Jesus? *John 8:31* gives the answer: "Then said Jesus to those Jews which believed on him, If ye continue in my word, then are ye my disciples indeed."

So, to say that I am a disciple of Jesus, I need first of all to come to Him and be willing to sit at His feet and receive from Him. I need also to apply His Word in my life by following His example and being willing to share what I have received with others. Jesus said in *Matthew 10:25*, "It is enough for the disciple that he be as his master, and the servant as his lord."

To help others become students (imitators) of Christ, I must first be taught to live the Christ life. One of the greatest problems of today's church is that many have not been properly trained in the Christ life. We can give only what we ourselves have received. *Mark 3:13-15* gives us a picture of how Jesus discipled His followers:

> And he goeth up into a mountain, and calleth unto him whom he would: and they came unto him.
> And he ordained twelve, that they should be with him, and that he might send them forth to preach, and to have power to heal sicknesses, and to cast out devils.

Successful discipleship is a blend of theory and practice. It is more than just going through a series of lessons. It is spending time with someone who carries the life of Christ, learning and doing, to the point where there is a transfer of this person's life into yours. It is receiving Life and pouring this Life you have received into others. It was in line with this that Paul instructed Timothy to pass on to others what he had received from him:

> And the things that thou hast heard of me among many witnesses, the same commit thou to faithful men, who shall be able to teach others also.
> *2 Timothy 2:2*

Can you imagine what the world would look like if we were all like Christ? That would be heaven on earth! Righteousness, peace and joy in the Holy Spirit would prevail everywhere (*Romans 14:17*). For this to become a reality, you have a key role to play. Allow yourself to be discipled. Then, become a disciple-maker yourself.

Someone has said that the only thing needed for evil to prevail is for good people to do nothing. We must do *something*: we must disciple people. The key to world transformation is effective discipleship. Receive the life of Christ, and start pouring that life into others—disciples who will in turn be faithful in pouring the Christ life they have received into other likeminded men and women, who will on their part do likewise, until the world is saturated with people carrying the life of Christ Jesus in them.

If you are committed to this, then you can declare:

**BECAUSE I AM DISCIPLED IN CHRIST,
I AM A DISCIPLE MAKER!**

Every tongue that rises in judgment against me, I condemn in Jesus' Name

No weapon that is formed against thee shall prosper; and every tongue that shall rise against thee in judgment thou shalt condemn.

Isaiah 54:17

Your wellbeing does not depend totally on God or on yourself, but it is a partnership. God delights in partnering with you, not because He cannot take care of you completely, but because He wants you to exercise the authority that He has given you. Listen to what Jesus has promised us in *Luke 10:19*:

> Behold, I give unto you power to tread on serpents and scorpions, and over all the power of the enemy: and nothing shall by any means hurt you.

Have you received the power God has given you? If not, receive it by faith now, so that you can condemn any tongue that rises in judgment against you. For it is the devil who is the accuser of the brethren:

> And I heard a loud voice saying in heaven, Now is come salvation, and strength, and the kingdom of our God, and the power of his Christ: for the accuser of our brethren is cast down, which accused them before our God day and night.

Revelation 12:10

Why would the enemy want to accuse us? Because words have the power to influence us either positively or negatively. The enemy knows that his words of accusation will affect us negatively. When God tells you to condemn every tongue that rises in judgment against you (*Isaiah 54:17b*), He is giving you the authority to refute the lies and accusations of the enemy. You have this authority because it is God who justifies you:

> Who shall bring a charge against God's elect? It is God who justifies. Who is he who condemns? It is Christ who died, and furthermore is also risen, who is even at the right hand of God, who also makes intercession for us.
>
> *Romans 8:33-34, NKJV*

No one can curse that which God has blessed. This was the message God had for Balak, when he wanted to curse the Israelites through Balaam: "Thou shalt not curse the people: for they are blessed" (*Numbers 22:12*).

At times we might lack the boldness to rebuke the enemy. Thank God that, by His grace, He reproaches Satan on our behalf at such times—as in the case of the high priest Joshua:

> And he shewed me Joshua the high priest standing before the angel of the LORD, and Satan standing at his right hand to resist him.
>
> And the LORD said unto Satan, The LORD rebuke thee, O Satan; even the LORD that hath chosen Jerusalem rebuke thee: is not this a brand plucked out of the fire?
>
> *Zechariah 3:1-2*

God can rebuke the devil on your behalf. But, because of the righteousness of Christ that you carry, you have the right and the authority to condemn every tongue that rises against you. This must be done audibly (see *Romans 10:9*).

Every time the devil attacks you with his lies, refute him with the Word of God. When he says you are a sinner, declare that you are the righteousness of God in Christ, according to *2 Corinthians 5:21*. When he calls you a failure, condemn that lie by declaring that you are a success because the Wonderful Counselor, Mighty God, Everlasting Father and Prince of Peace lives in you, according to *Isaiah 9:6*.

To refute the enemy's lies, you need to know the Word of God. The Bible says that you shall know the truth, and the truth you know and apply will set you free (*John 8:31-32, 36; James 2:17*). As you condemn every tongue that rises against you, either from the devil himself or from man, victory will be yours. David understood this principle and slew God's enemies with His Word before he even slew them physically:

> And the Philistine said unto David, Am I a dog, that thou comest to me with staves? And the Philistine cursed David by his gods. Then said David to the Philistine, Thou comest to me with a sword, and with a spear, and with a shield: but I come to thee in the name of the LORD of hosts, the God of the armies of Israel, whom thou hast defied.
>
> This day will the LORD deliver thee into mine hand; and I will smite thee, and take thine head from thee; and I will give the carcases of the host of the Philistines this day unto the fowls of the air, and to the wild beasts of the earth... for the battle is the LORD's, and he will give you into our hands.
>
> *1 Samuel 17:45-47*

Slay your enemies with the Word of God and declare with confidence today:

EVERY TONGUE THAT RISES IN JUDGMENT AGAINST ME, I CONDEMN IN JESUS' NAME!

Because I walk in the righteousness of Jesus, my prayers produce results

The effectual fervent prayer of a righteous man availeth much.

James 5:16(b)

For our prayers to produce outstanding results, three elements are crucial: **effectiveness**, **fervency** and **righteousness**. But, before we examine these three factors, we need to define prayer.

What is prayer? For many people, prayer is all about asking God for things or talking to Him. But it is much more than that: it is talking *with* God. We are lightened, excited and fulfilled when we share our deepest feelings and thoughts with God and when He in turn tells us what is on His mind and in His heart. His words are sweeter to our spirits than honey. Nothing else in life is more satisfying than this intimate relationship we have with God. The Psalmist has said:

Thou wilt shew me the path of life: in thy presence is fullness of joy; at thy right hand there are pleasures for evermore.

Psalm 16:11

We talk with God in prayer, and He talks to us mainly through His Word. We can therefore define prayer as fellowshipping with God or having a heart-to-heart dialogue with Him.

When we talk of *effective* prayers, we are talking about prayers based on the Word of God. Through the Word of God, we are able to know the mind of God. Effective prayer is also disciplined prayer. It is developing the right habits that permit us to be in good shape to seek God; it is identifying the appropriate environment and time to communicate well with God. Daniel, for example, made it his habit to seek God at three specific times a day (see *Daniel 6:10*).

Effective praying also involves fasting. Fasting is not trying to force the hand of God to do things for us. Fasting is spiritual emphasis—taking time off to concentrate on God. It will usually involve staying away from all forms of pleasure so that we can focus on seeking God. This discipline permits us to hear God more clearly and to respond to Him better.

Fervency in prayer speaks of consistency. It is making prayer our lifestyle. It is loving the presence of God so much that we desire to talk with Him at all times. It is praying without ceasing (*1 Thessalonians 5:17*): Pray Until Something Happens (PUSH). This speaks of faith and perseverance. Elijah set us an example of fervency when he prayed seven times for rain before the rain clouds showed up. He never gave up until he got what he wanted (*1 Kings 18:42-45*).

Righteousness speaks of right standing with God. Sin separates us from God:

> Behold, the LORD's hand is not shortened, that it cannot save; neither his ear heavy, that it cannot hear: But your iniquities have separated between you and your God, and your sins have hid his face from you, that he will not hear.
>
> *Isaiah 59:1-2*

If the issue of sin is not dealt with, our prayers will not produce results. *Psalm 66:18* says, "If I regard iniquity in my heart, the LORD will not hear me."

God does not hear the prayers of a sinner (*John 9:31*), unless the sinner repents and asks Jesus into his or her heart. The key to being sure God will hear you is to be sure you are born again into God's Kingdom. Are you born again? Is Jesus your LORD and GOD? If yes, you have the right to talk with your Father. If not, take a look at *Acts 2:36-39*.

When we receive Christ, there is an exchange: He takes away our sinful life and gives us His righteous life. It is this gift of righteousness we have received that makes it possible for us to stand boldly before God and talk with Him and see results in our lives. *Hebrews 4:16* exhorts us: "Let us therefore come boldly unto the throne of grace, that we may obtain mercy, and find grace to help in time of need."

So, when we talk with God based on the fact that we are righteous in Christ, and when we pray boldly, effectively and fervently, we will see positive results that bring glory to His name. We will see Him move mountains in our lives, families, jobs, businesses and ministries. *1 John 5:14-15* tells us:

> And this is the confidence that we have in him, that, if we ask any thing according to his will, he heareth us: and if we know that he hear us, whatsoever we ask, we know that we have the petitions that we desired of him.

You can talk with God without having to pass through any protocol. Are you taking advantage of the prayer platform He has given you? If you have prayed, but you do not see immediate results, do not be discouraged. Give God the glory that you have been heard. Start giving thanks to Him before you see the physical manifestation. Giving thanks to God in advance is a sign of faith. With this in mind, you can declare:

BECAUSE I WALK IN THE RIGHTEOUSNESS OF JESUS, MY PRAYERS PRODUCE RESULTS!

I am a lender and not a borrower

For the LORD thy God blesseth thee, as he promised thee: and thou shalt lend unto many nations, but thou shalt not borrow; and thou shalt reign over many nations, but they shall not reign over thee.

Deuteronomy 15:6

God's desire from the onset has always been for His children to have the best of everything. Though borrowing is not a sin, it is not God's best for us. The rich rule over the poor, and the borrower is a servant to the lender (*Proverbs 22:7*). The world system encourages borrowing because the lenders know what they can make from the borrowers. But how can we pay our bills without having to borrow, in a world where the economy has gone sour? It is indeed difficult.

These days, to possess a house of our own, own a car, send children to school, or realize any serious project, we find ourselves compelled to borrow. The question we need to ask is: *what did the lender do to have that which we don't— money to lend?* The answer is that he must have worked hard, or someone else did the hard work and left him an inheritance.

Jesus once remarked that, when it comes to doing business, "the children of this world are in their generation wiser than the children of light" (*Luke 16:8*). The world system has its own wisdom by which it operates. James describes worldly wisdom as being sensual, devilish and full of envy, strife, confusion and every evil work (*James 3:15-16*).

As children of God and citizens of His Kingdom, we have our own economic system, which far surpasses the system of the world. We operate according to the wisdom and favour that is from above:

> But the wisdom that is from above is first pure, then peaceable, gentle, and easy to be intreated, full of mercy and good fruits, without partiality, and without hypocrisy.
>
> *James 3:17*

Because we live in a sinful world, we need God's supernatural intervention if we are to successfully operate His economic system here on earth. In *Deuteronomy 8:18*, God revealed the blueprint for His system to the children of Israel:

> But thou shalt remember the LORD thy God: for it is he that *giveth thee power to get wealth*, that he may establish his covenant which he sware unto thy fathers, as it is this day.

To be lenders and not borrowers, we need to understand how God empowers His people. He empowers us through:

- *Conception* of ideas (*Genesis 26:1-3*)
- *Connection* with the right people (*Genesis 26:19*)
- *Currency*, the seed to start with (*2 Corinthians 9:8-11*)
- *Concretization*, the planting of the seed, leading to fruitfulness, multiplication, replenishing and subduing (*Genesis 1:28*)

In line with all this, Jesus has given us this assurance:

> He that believeth on me, as the scripture hath said, out of his belly shall flow rivers of living water.
>
> *John 7:38*

The rivers of living water are first and foremost ideas on how you can be a blessing to humanity. In God's economy, the profit motive is not dominant. Rather, the concern is to find out how you can be a source of blessing to others. As we seek to bless others, we get blessed ourselves. Most often, it is through our God-given talents that we bless others—and then we get blessed in return.

Once we are blessed, we become a perpetual source of blessing to others, and borrowing will be automatically stamped out of our lives. This might sound simplistic, but God told His children that, as long as they operated under His open heaven, they were bound to be lenders and not borrowers:

> The LORD shall open unto thee his good treasure, the heaven to give the rain unto thy land in his season, and to bless all the work of thine hand: and thou shalt lend unto many nations, and thou shalt not borrow.
>
> *Deuteronomy 28:12*

Are you currently a lender or a borrower? If you are a borrower, I guarantee you that your story will change if you follow these principles:

- Call on God today to empower you with the right ideas, to connect you with the right people, and to release unto you the right seeds and opportunities to sow these seeds;

- Ask Him to water the seeds you have planted; and

- Trust Him for the increase.

Remember, it was in the midst of a famine that Isaac prospered (*Genesis 26:12-14*). You are next in line. Declare with confidence today and always that:

I AM A LENDER AND NOT A BORROWER!

I achieve extraordinary results because the One who is greater than Solomon lives in me

The queen of Sheba shall rise against this nation in the judgment and condemn it; for she came from a distant land to hear the wisdom of Solomon; and now one greater than Solomon is here—and you refuse to believe him.

Matthew 12:42, TLB

Jesus is the One who is "greater than Solomon". Solomon was a marvel in his day. Kings and queens—among them, the Queen of Sheba (*1 Kings 10:1-13*)—were awed by his God-given wisdom and wealth. Jesus, on the other hand, was scorned by the people of His day, especially by the scribes and Pharisees. They failed to discern that someone greater than Solomon was among them.

Jesus termed them an evil and adulterous generation (*Matthew 12:39*), remarking that the Queen of Sheba would condemn them at the Judgment. It is sad when people fail to see Jesus as the One who is "greater than Solomon"; they are missing out on so much. However, if you have received Christ into your life, "one greater than Solomon" now lives in you.

What this means for you is that the wisdom and wealth Solomon manifested is now your portion—and in an even greater measure, for He who gave Solomon what he had is now residing in you! It is possible for us to manifest a greater

85

glory than Solomon manifested, but we have to be willing to do what Solomon did—and even more—to provoke the release of God's glory in our lives, as he did. We are told that Solomon offered God "a thousand burnt offerings" (*1 Kings 3:4*). His offering provoked heaven so much so that God appeared to him that very night and asked Solomon what he wanted.

Solomon asked God for wisdom to rule His people, and God was so pleased with him for asking the right thing that He gave Solomon the wisdom he had asked for and, on top of that, what he had not asked for—riches and honour. He also promised to give him a long life if he continued to walk in God's ways (*1 Kings 3:4-14*). Solomon caused kings and queens to marvel at his God. Though he compromised his faith later in his life, he did leave a great impact. The Queen of Sheba, for example, was dumfounded when she saw Solomon's glory.

If you are willing to give to God sacrificially, as Solomon did, God will not be indifferent to your gift. The greatest gift we can give to God, however, is our very selves. Are you willing to cause men to marvel at your God? If you follow Solomon's example, you will certainly enjoy extraordinary results, because One greater than Solomon is residing in you.

It is our responsibility to cause men to marvel at our God. The potential is already within us, but we have to release it through our actions. We are of the latter house, and the Lord says that the glory of the latter house shall be greater than the glory of the former (*Haggai 2:9*). The results we reap will depend on our vision. God wants us to reap extraordinary results so that we can:

- Enjoy His blessings (*1 Timothy 6:17; Proverbs 10:22*)
- Be a blessing to others (*Genesis 12:1-3*)
- Bring glory to the name of the Lord (*1 Kings 10:1-13*)
- Help further God's Kingdom (*Romans 10:14-15*)

The world has mocked at our Jesus for too long. We must manifest extraordinary results so that God's people will not be seen as poverty-stricken beggars. It has been said that the wisdom of the poor is despised (*Ecclesiastes 9:16*) and that money is the answer to everything (*Ecclesiastes 10:19*). We are talking here about money on assignment; not money to show off, but to advance God's Kingdom. After all, He says that the silver and gold are His (*Haggai 2:8*).

As God lavishes you with wealth and wisdom in these end times, you will manifest extraordinary results. We will see, in the newspapers, headlines like the following...

- *Good News! Good News! A Christian Business Magnate Puts Smiles on the Faces of Orphans!*

- *Christian Multi-Billionaire Brings Hope to Widows!*

- *New Christian University with State-of-the-Art Facilities Goes Operational!*

All this may sound far-fetched, but it is already happening! In these last days, we are going to see a great transfer of wealth from the wicked to the righteous, so that God's children can enjoy extraordinary results (*Job 27:16-17; Ecclesiastes 2:26; Proverbs 13:22, 28:8; Isaiah 23:17-18*).

Forget about mediocrity, timidity and inferiority! We are here to make a difference and make it in grand style! The world will be in awe, like the Queen of Sheba in the days of Solomon. For the church, the best is yet to be. The world will see what it has never seen before. It will marvel as you manifest extraordinary results. Jesus is coming for a glorious Church, not a weak and miserable bride.

With all this in mind, you can declare with confidence:

I ACHIEVE EXTRAORDINARY RESULTS BECAUSE THE ONE WHO IS GREATER THAN SOLOMON LIVES IN ME!

I am a victor and not a victim

For whatsoever is born of God overcometh the world: and this is the victory that overcometh the world, even our faith.

1 John 5:4

In a world filled with all kinds of challenges, we may at times feel like we are losers: that life has turned us into victims, not victors. Where I come from (Africa), we seem to be more victims than victors of our circumstances, caught up in a web of poverty, joblessness, juvenile delinquency, social injustice and strife, political oppression and instability, terrorism, war, refugee crises, cybercrimes, malnutrition, epidemics and more.

We are not alone, however; the Bible records many occasions when God's people have also felt like victims and not victors. Habakkuk at one point cried out to God:

> O LORD, how long shall I cry, and thou wilt not hear! Even cry out unto thee of violence, and thou wilt not save!
>
> Why dost thou shew me iniquity, and cause me to behold grievance? For spoiling and violence are before me: and there are that raise up strife and contention.
>
> Therefore the law is slacked, and judgment doth never go forth: for the wicked doth compass about the righteous; therefore wrong judgment proceedeth.
>
> *Habakkuk 1:2-4*

And in *Psalm 73* we have a lament by the Psalmist Asaph, who envied the wicked and saw himself as a failure.

Verily I have cleansed my heart in vain, and washed my hands in innocency. For all the day long have I been plagued, and chastened every morning.

Psalm 73:13-14

But, though the wicked might seem to prosper in life, there is nothing to envy about them. Both Asaph and Habakkuk came to understand this later, as their declarations showed:

When I thought to know this, it was too painful for me; Until I went into the sanctuary of God; then understood I their end. Surely thou didst set them in slippery places: thou castedst them down into destruction.

Psalm 73:16-18

Although the fig tree shall not blossom, neither shall fruit be in the vines... Yet I will rejoice in the LORD, I will joy in the God of my salvation. The LORD God is my strength, and he will make my feet like hinds' feet, and he will make me to walk upon mine high places.

Habakkuk 3:17-19

It is this kind of understanding that enables us to declare along with them: "We are victors and not victims!" For our victory is based not so much on our performance as our strong belief that Jesus has overcome the world for us. Therefore, we are no longer slaves to the world system. Through faith in Christ, we have victory over the lust of the flesh, the lust of the eyes, and the boastful pride of this world (*1 John 2:15-17*).

The Bible assures us that, though we may have many troubles, the Lord will deliver us from them all (*Psalm 34:19*). Our Lord exhorts us to be of good cheer in the face of trouble, for He has overcome the world (*John 16:33*). Because of what Jesus has done, you can declare with confidence:

I AM A VICTOR AND NOT A VICTIM!

Because I am reconciled with God, I am His ambassador

God was in Christ, reconciling the world unto himself, not imputing their trespasses unto them; and hath committed unto us the word of reconciliation. Now then we are ambassadors for Christ, as though God did beseech you by us: we pray you in Christ's stead, be ye reconciled to God.

2 Corinthians 5:19-20

An ambassador is a minister who represents his government in a foreign country. In the same way, as ambassadors for Christ, we are His ministers (servants), representing His Kingdom on planet earth. This means that, if anyone wants to know more about the Kingdom of God, it will be through us.

Our main assignment as Christ's ambassadors is to reconcile people to God, so that they can enjoy all that God's Kingdom has to offer and bring Him glory as they live for Him—while helping to reconcile others to Him too!

We are vessels in God's hands; He does the reconciliation through us. And, just like the world's ambassadors, we are endowed with all we need to fulfill our assignment. Our greatest endowment is the Spirit of God Himself:

But you will receive power when the Holy Spirit comes on you; and you will be my witnesses in Jerusalem, and in all Judea and Samaria, and to the ends of the earth.

Acts 1:8, NIV

This is such an exciting responsibility, to be the representative of the most glorious Kingdom that ever existed! We need to carry ourselves with dignity, as the world's ambassadors do. But how do we go about this exciting—albeit delicate—assignment that can also be challenging at times?

First, we need to ensure that we ourselves belong to God's Kingdom. Then, when the opportunity presents itself—as led by the Spirit of God—we need to explain to people clearly and biblically how they can be reconciled with God in order to have eternal life and enjoy a fulfilling life while on earth; this brings glory to God (*1 John 5:11-13; John 10:10; 1 Peter 2:9*).

God's plan of salvation and reconciliation with Him has been clearly laid out in *Acts 2:36-39*:

> Therefore let all the house of Israel know assuredly, that God hath made the same Jesus, whom ye have crucified, both Lord and Christ.
>
> Now when they heard this, they were pricked in their heart, and said unto Peter and to the rest of the apostles, Men and brethren, what shall we do?
>
> Then Peter said unto them, Repent, and be baptized every one of you in the name of Jesus Christ for the remission of sins, and ye shall receive the gift of the Holy Ghost. For the promise is unto you, and to your children, and to all that are afar off, even as many as the Lord our God shall call.

Five points stand out here:

1. Recognize who Jesus Christ is (*John 17:3*)
2. Repent
3. Receive Jesus Christ into your life
4. Receive water baptism in Jesus' Name
5. Receive the Baptism of the Holy Spirit

Many people base their salvation on the wrong premise, thinking that all it takes is to go to church, try to keep the Ten Commandments, try to do good, participate in church activities, and so on. All this is good, but it is not enough—as Jesus made it clear to Nicodemus when He told him that, to see the Kingdom of God, one must be born again of God's Spirit (*John 3:1-5*). To enter the Kingdom of God, one must be born of water and of the Spirit.

Those who followed Jesus while He was on earth wanted to know what God's will was. He answered, "This is the will of God, that you believe in the one he has sent" (*John 6:29, TLB*). To the Pharisees of His day, Jesus said, "Unless you believe that I am the Messiah, the Son of God, you will die in your sins" (*John 8:24, TLB*).

To believe in Jesus is to know who He really is. Our Lord did not hesitate to ask His disciples who they thought He was. Peter got the right answer:

> And Simon Peter answered and said, Thou art the Christ, the Son of the living God.
>
> *Matthew 16:16*

The word *Christ* means "the Anointed One; "the Liberator". "Son of the living God" does not mean God gave birth to Jesus or that God created Jesus, as some erroneously think. "Son of the living God" means the image or manifestation of the living God (*Colossians 1:13-16*). Jesus is God in human form. Thomas called Him "my Lord and my God" (*John 20:28*), and Paul also proclaimed Him as God manifested in the flesh:

> And without controversy great is the mystery of godliness: God was manifest in the flesh, justified in the Spirit, seen of angels, preached unto the Gentiles, believed on in the world, received up into glory.
>
> *1 Timothy 3:16*

Jesus is one hundred percent God and one hundred percent Man. As God, He is Spirit (*John 4:24*). As Spirit, He could not die for man; He needed a body to do so. That was why He came into the world through Mary's womb. As the angel declared:

> And she shall bring forth a son, and thou shalt call his name Jesus: for he shall save his people from their sins...
>
> Behold, a virgin shall be with child, and shall bring forth a son, and they shall call his name Emmanuel, which being interpreted is, God with us.
>
> *Matthew 1:21, 23*

Jesus is the Word that was from the beginning, that became flesh and dwelt among men (*John 1:14*). God became a man just to save you. How dare you take that for granted?

It is only when you know Jesus personally, for who He really is, that you can begin to relate rightly with Him. After knowing Jesus Christ to be the God-Man, the next thing that follows is repentance.

What is repentance? This is another word that many misinterpret. Many think it is about confessing or listing our sins or being sorry for our sins. But we can't even remember all our sins to begin with, let alone confess them.

"Repentance" comes from the Greek word *metanoeo*, which means "to think differently or afterwards; to reconsider (morally); to feel compunction". To repent is to acknowledge that one was headed in the wrong direction and to make a U-turn to head in the right direction.

The fruit of repentance is a change in behavior. Jesus, John, Peter and Paul all preached repentance (*Mark 1:4; Matthew 4:17; Acts 2:38, 20:21*). Unless we change our minds about Jesus and ourselves, we cannot accommodate Him or what He has to offer (*Hosea 4:6*), which is why He said that new wine cannot be put in old wineskins (*Matthew 9:17*).

Repentance needs to be followed by inviting Christ into one's life as one's Lord and Saviour; as *John 1:12-13* says:

> But as many as received him, to them gave he power to become the sons of God, even to them that believe on his name: Which were born, not of blood, nor of the will of the flesh, nor of the will of man, but of God.

We receive Jesus by grace through faith (*Ephesians 2: 8-9*). Faith is manifested through prayer. The Bible assures us:

> That if thou shalt confess with thy mouth the Lord Jesus, and shalt believe in thine heart that God hath raised him from the dead, thou shalt be saved.
> For with the heart man believeth unto righteousness; and with the mouth confession is made unto salvation.
>
> *Romans 10:9-10*

All who believe in Christ should be invited to ask Him into their lives. Here is a proposed prayer:

> LORD JESUS, *I acknowledge You as the Christ, the Son of the Living God. I repent of my wrongful thoughts toward You and myself.4 Thank You for dying for my sins. I confess with my mouth that You are my Lord and my God. I believe that You died and rose again for me. I receive You into my Spirit, and I declare that I am born again. I am now a child of God. I have eternal life. Fill me with Your Holy Spirit and help me to follow You daily.*
> *In Jesus' Name, Amen.*

---

4 To repent (*Acts 2:38*) is to change my mind about who Christ is and who I am: to acknowledge that Jesus is GOD and not just a servant of God or just another great Prophet or Teacher. If I don't recognize Jesus as God and the Son of God, I will die in my sins (*John 8:24*). Concerning who I am, I must start seeing myself as God sees me—loved and forgiven by Him—and I will then act as such: for, as a man thinks in his heart, so is he (*Proverbs 23:7*). When I sincerely change and start to think right thoughts about Christ and myself, my actions will follow suit.

This prayer of commitment is made once and for all of one's lifetime. We need to follow this up by guiding believers to take the next step of being baptized in water, which is the external manifestation of their inward change. Baptism is a message we preach publicly, that we are crucified with Christ, we are buried with Him, and we are resurrected with Him.

> In baptism we show that we have been saved from death and doom by the resurrection of Christ; not because our bodies are washed clean by the water but because in being baptized we are turning to God and asking him to cleanse our hearts from sin.
>
> *1 Peter 3:21, TLB*

The word "baptism" comes from the Greek *baptizo*, which means "to immerse, submerge; to make whelmed (fully wet)". All who believe in Jesus are immersed in His Name, for salvation is found in no other name but His (*Acts 4:10-12*). For other references to baptism in the Name of Jesus, check out *Acts 8:5, 12, 16; 10:48; 19:1-5*.

Thereafter, we also need to tell people about the baptism of the Holy Spirit. This is the Spirit of God inhabiting and empowering those who have received the word of Christ. Believers in Christ should desire and ask for the baptism of the Holy Spirit (*Matthew 5:6*), which will enable them to live the Christ life and make a difference for Him. God assures us:

> "So if you sinful people know how to give good gifts to your children, how much more will your heavenly Father give the Holy Spirit to those who ask him."
>
> *Luke 11:13, NLT*

Those who have received the baptism of the Holy Spirit often manifest it by speaking in an unknown tongue (*Acts 2:1-4,*

10:44-47, 19:6). It is our responsibility to pray for people who have received Christ, that they be baptized by His Spirit—after which they need to seek to be filled regularly (*Ephesians 5:18*). Once one has received the baptism and filling of the Holy Spirit, the fruit of the Spirit will also be evident (*Galatians 5:16-24*).

These are the steps people need to take, to be born into God's family. From thence, you need to help them identify with a living church where they can continue to grow in Christ and be of service in His Kingdom (see *Acts 2:42-47, 4:32-37*).

From start to finish in this work of reconciling people to God, you can declare with confidence:

BECAUSE I AM RECONCILED WITH GOD, I AM HIS AMBASSADOR ON EARTH!

I am blessed to bless

I will make of thee a great nation, and I will bless thee, and make thy name great; and thou shalt be a blessing: And I will bless them that bless thee, and curse him that curseth thee: and in thee shall all families of the earth be blessed.

Genesis 12:2-3

The promises of God usually seem too good to be true. This is because He is more than good. He "is able to do exceedingly abundantly above all that we ask or think, according to the power that works in us" (*Ephesians 3:20, NKJV*).

When God looks at you, He sees your destiny as a whole. He sees into your future and calls you what you will become as though you *are* already what He says you are.

That is what the Scriptures mean when they say that God made Abraham the father of many nations. God will accept all people in every nation who trust God as Abraham did. And this promise is from God himself, who makes the dead live again and speaks of future events with as much certainty as though they were already past.

Romans 4:17, TLB

Abraham became the father of many nations. The one whose wife was past the age of childbearing became the source of many nations. The one who had no name in his family became a name to be respected. He who was poor became more than rich.

If you are in Christ, you are blessed. You don't need to feel or look blessed to be blessed. What God promised to Abraham is yours too.

And now that we are Christ's we are the true descendants of Abraham, and **all of God's promises to him belong to us**.

Galatians 3:29, TLB

To be blessed is to be favored and empowered by God. It is this supernatural ability that attracts blessings to us—a good spouse, children, houses, health, wealth, and so on. But the greatest blessing you can possess and you can give the world is Jesus. In Christ are hidden all the treasures of God.

Most often we think we must have material things to be a blessing to others. That is not true. Material things are important, but the one thing needful is the Word of God, because in the Word is Life, and this Life is the Light of the world.

Stop seeing yourself as someone who has nothing to offer. Learn how to share your faith with others. The next time you hear there is training being conducted somewhere on how to share your faith, do not hesitate to go for it. Jesus said to those He called, "Follow me, and I will make you fishers of men" (*Matthew 4:19*).

When you see yourself as one who has been blessed by God, you will begin to realize that you have an awesome responsibility to be a blessing to others too. Paul exhorts us to "remember the words of the Lord Jesus, how he said, It is more blessed to give than to receive" (*Acts 20:35b*).

As you seek to bless people spiritually and in other ways, God will in turn bless you even more. So, no matter what your present circumstances are, whether you feel blessed or not right now, begin to declare with confidence that:

I AM BLESSED TO BLESS!

As I excel in many virtues, I also excel in the grace of giving

But since you excel in everything—in faith, in speech, in knowledge, in complete earnestness and in the love we have kindled in you—see that you also excel in this grace of giving.

2 Corinthians 8:7, NIV

The story is told of a dog that was crossing a bridge with a bone in its mouth. As it looked into the stream below, it saw what looked like another dog in the water, carrying a similar bone. Out of greed and jealousy, the dog on the bridge quickly dived into the water to grab the other dog's bone. But what it did not know was that the other dog was only its own reflection in the stream. So, the dog lost its bone and got a good soaking—all because of its greed and jealousy!

Humans have a natural tendency to hoard too. It is not easy to part with stuff—whether it's our money or material goods. This tendency is the result of sin in our hearts. We are afraid of what will become of us if we give away our wealth. The rich want to grow richer and widen the gap between them and the poor. This is true even of Christians. It has been said that many Christians get baptized, but their wallets are not baptized!

Does this mean we can't save or keep anything for ourselves? Far from it. Our progress in the grace of giving is measured by what we give, not what we keep. Ask yourself: what is the proportion of what you give to what you keep?

Paul exhorted the Corinthians to excel in the grace of giving because he knew this did not come naturally. In fact, he once told the Philippians, "not one church shared with me in the matter of giving... except you only" (*Philippians 4:15*). While some do have the gift of generosity (*Romans 12:8*), Paul's appeal in *2 Corinthians 8:7* is for *all* to desire to excel in giving, even as we excel in other virtues. As someone has said, any revival that does not touch the pocket is no revival at all!

What does it mean to *excel* in the grace of giving? It means to go beyond the ordinary, to do better than others, to be very good and surpass others in our ability to give. We need to excel in our giving for the advancement of God's Kingdom. We need to excel in our giving to the poor and needy, to the widows and orphans. God has blessed us for a purpose: that we might be a blessing to others, so that they will come to Him.

How can we excel in this grace of giving? First, *desire* to excel in giving. Then ask God for help to follow His leadership as He opens up opportunities for us to give. Following God's leadership requires faith on our part, as in Abraham's case when God asked him to offer Isaac to Him (*Genesis 22:1-18*).

God is the greatest Giver ever, and He set an example for us to follow. *John 3:16* says, "For God so loved the world, that he gave his only begotten Son, that whosoever believeth in him should not perish, but have everlasting life." We can give without loving, but we can't love without giving. Our giving is a practical demonstration of our love for God and faith in Him.

We are not to give out of pressure or to be seen. Neither are we to give our leftovers, what we don't need. Instead, we should give our best, giving ourselves first. We should give as much as God has blessed us, and give it cheerfully and only to worthy causes, sowing on fertile ground (*2 Corinthians 8:1-7, 9:6-15*).

Why must I excel in this grace of giving? Because it is a command from God: "Give, and it shall be given unto you"

(*Luke 6:38*). It is the key to our blessings. We shouldn't give just to be blessed but, when we give rightly, we will surely be blessed. Our needs will always be more than our resources: so, when you have a need, sow a seed to meet it. The harvest you enjoy today is the seed you sowed yesterday. The harvest you will have tomorrow depends on the seed you sow today.

Examples abound of people who have experienced the wonders of excelling in the grace of giving. Abel gave the best of his flock, and this pleased God (*Genesis 4:4*). Noah offered the best to God after the flood, and God promised never again to destroy the world with water (*Genesis 8:20-22*). Abraham gave Isaac, and God blessed him and his descendants greatly and also blessed the world through his seed (*Genesis 22:1-18*). Solomon gave 1000 burnt offerings, and God gave him a blank check (*1 Kings 3:1-5*). The case of David in *2 Samuel 24:24-25* is also worthy of note: he refused to offer sacrifices that cost him nothing but paid the price for them, and God answered his prayers and withdrew the plague from the land of Israel.

The early Church gave generously, and there were no needy persons among them. The Lord increased their number, and they enjoyed His great grace (*Acts 2:42-47, 4:32-37*). The Macedonians gave out of their extreme poverty, and God gave them more grace (*2 Corinthians 8:1-5*).

Apart from these examples, many people today have also testified to the joy of excelling in the grace of giving. One man decided to give God ninety percent of his earnings, and God turned things around for him so that what he had left was still more than enough for him to live on. God is faithful. He will not ask us to do anything that will not benefit us.

How is your giving today? If you desire to excel in the grace of giving, start declaring with confidence:

AS I EXCEL IN MANY VIRTUES, I ALSO EXCEL IN THE GRACE OF GIVING!

As Jesus was, so am I growing strong in spirit, mind and body

And the Child grew and became strong in spirit, filled with wisdom; and the grace of God was upon Him.

Luke 2:40, NKJV

And Jesus increased in wisdom and stature, and in favour with God and man.

Luke 2:52

You were created for progress. God gave you a mind that must be developed, a body that must be strengthened, a spirit that must be nourished, and relationships that must be built. Many people grow in a one-sided manner. Some are brilliant intellectuals but have no favour with God or man. Some are in good shape physically, but they have no wisdom; nor have they developed sound relationships.

How can we grow and increase, as Jesus did, in wisdom and stature and in favor with God and man? Growing in wisdom is growing in the fear of God, for the fear of the Lord is the beginning of wisdom (*Proverbs 1:7*). To grow in the fear of God requires growth in the knowledge of God. God has revealed Himself to us in His Word and in daily life. Writing to Timothy, Paul had this to say in *2 Timothy 3:15:*

And that from a child thou hast known the holy scriptures, which are able to make thee wise unto salvation through faith which is in Christ Jesus.

The Word of God is our best source of wisdom. It reveals to us who God is and what He expects from us. Those who, by the help of God's Spirit, receive revelations from God and respond accordingly are recognized as wise. As Jesus has said:

> Therefore everyone who hears these words of mine and puts them into practice is like a wise man who built his house on the rock.
>
> *Matthew 7:24, NIV*

This means that whoever walks in integrity, love, faithfulness, generosity, and all else that Jesus teaches us to do, is being wise. Whatever you do in obedience to His Word is for your own good. It is an investment you are making in yourself. To be ignorant of God's Word—and to continue in ignorance by neglecting to study the Bible—or to know the Word and not do it is to be foolish.

To refuse to have faith in God or know His power is to be foolish (*Matthew 22:29*). To deny His existence is to be even more foolish; *Psalm 14:1* says, "The fool hath said in his heart, There is no God." But the wise will seek to bring such lost souls to Christ. *Proverbs 11:30* tells us, "he that winneth souls is wise". Therefore, when you are busy winning souls for God's Kingdom, you are being wise.

Obedience to God leads not only to growth in wisdom but peace with Him too. Peace with God, along with eating and resting well and exercising regularly, results naturally in good physical health. You need to be physically fit to serve God.

As you live in obedience to God, you will also attract His favour to yourself. And, the more you have of God's favour, the more you become an attraction to others. People will be automatically attracted to you because you carry something special within you. Your presence will bless those who have faith in God, but it will also offend the enemies of God.

And the whole multitude sought to touch him: for there went virtue out of him, and healed them all.

Luke 6:19

Jesus grew in favour with men because, everywhere He went, He was doing good:

God anointed Jesus of Nazareth with the Holy Spirit and with power, who went about doing good and healing all who were oppressed by the devil, for God was with Him.

Acts 10:38, NKJV

We too can go about doing good—as Jesus did—when we are anointed with the Holy Spirit and with His power. This is made possible as we seek to "be filled with the [Holy] Spirit and constantly guided by Him" (*Ephesians 5:18, AMP*) on a daily basis.

How are you growing? No matter what stage of growth we are at, God commands us to grow in *all* dimensions so that we can live fruitful lives and bring glory to His Name:

You did not choose Me, but I chose you and appointed you that you should go and bear fruit, and that your fruit should remain, that whatever you ask the Father in My name He may give you.

John 15:16, NKJV

Above all else, grow in the grace and knowledge of OUR LORD AND SAVIOUR JESUS CHRIST (*2 Peter 3:18*). If you are seeking to grow in the grace and knowledge of our Lord and seeking to grow like Him, you can declare with confidence:

AS JESUS WAS, SO AM I GROWING STRONG IN SPIRIT, MIND AND BODY!

Because I believe in Christ Jesus, rivers of living water flow from within me

"Whoever believes in me, as Scripture has said, rivers of living water will flow from within them." By this he meant the Spirit, whom those who believed in him were later to receive.

John 7:38-39, NIV

But whosoever drinketh of the water that I shall give him shall never thirst; but the water that I shall give him shall be in him a well of water springing up into everlasting life.

John 4:14

Water is life. Without water, life on earth would be unlivable. Just as water is essential for physical life, the Holy Spirit of Christ is indispensable for a blessed life. Jesus has assured us that rivers of living water will flow from within all who believe in Him. These rivers of living water refer to the diverse blessings flowing from the spring or well of water which is the Holy Spirit dwelling within believers.

As these blessings flow out of Spirit-filled believers, all who come in touch with them will certainly be blessed. They will be blessed by the fruit, the qualities, and the gifts of the Holy Spirit of Christ. The fruit of the Spirit, according to *Galatians 5:22-23*, is love, joy, peace, patience, kindness, goodness, faithfulness, gentleness and self-control.

105

The qualities of the Spirit are listed in *Isaiah 11:2* as the Spirit of the Lord, the Spirit of wisdom, the Spirit of understanding, the Spirit of counsel, the Spirit of might, the Spirit of knowledge and the Spirit of the fear of the Lord.

The gifts of the Spirit, according to *1 Corinthians 12:8-10, Romans 12:6-8, Ephesians 4:11* and *1 Peter 4:10-11*, are "the word of wisdom", "the word of knowledge", faith, "gifts of healing", "working of miracles", prophecy, "discerning of spirits", "divers kinds of tongues", "interpretation of tongues", ministering, teaching, exhortation, generosity, leadership, mercy, and special abilities to function as apostles, prophets, evangelists, pastors or teachers.

With such an abundance of fruit, qualities and gifts of the Spirit, it is clear that every child of God is really a fountain of blessing to others. It is important to note that the fruit is in the singular; we don't talk of "the fruits" of the Holy Spirit but THE FRUIT. The fruit is from one source. You can't have one without the other, because a good tree produces only one kind of fruit. If the tree is good, all it produces has to be good.

The fruit, the gifts and the qualities of the Spirit all work together in a perfect blend. It is the love of Christ that compels us to evangelize. When we evangelize, the power of God's Spirit is made manifest through the gift of prophecy or miracles. Once people are born again, the Spirit of knowledge and the gift of teaching are there to assist us in the building of the saints. As needs are made manifest and met, we become really the salt of the earth and the light of the world, and God is glorified through us. It is in line with this that Peter says:

> But also for this very reason, giving all diligence, add to your faith virtue, to virtue knowledge, to knowledge self-control, to self-control perseverance, to perseverance godliness, to godliness brotherly kindness, and to brotherly kindness love.

106

> For if these things are yours and abound, you will be neither barren nor unfruitful in the knowledge of our Lord Jesus Christ.
>
> *2 Peter 1:5-8, NKJV*

As long as we are inhabited and empowered by God's Spirit, we can never and should never be unproductive. We are multi-faceted and creative. We are multi-talented. We are able to manifest diverse abilities through which we can bring people into God's Kingdom.

The world is like a wilderness, with many thirsting spiritually and physically. We are here to refresh them with the living water of God's blessings. Jesus showed us the way, teaching people the Word and multiplying five loaves and two fishes to feed the multitudes (*John 6:1-14; Matthew 14:15-20*). Though some followed Jesus for the loaves, He made them understand that they were to seek Him, not because of the food He provided, but for who He was (*Matthew 6:33*).

Apart from preaching, teaching and showing mercy, Jesus performed miracles like healing the sick, delivering the captives, and raising the dead back to life. *Acts 10:38* tells us:

> God anointed Jesus of Nazareth with the Holy Ghost and with power: who went about doing good, and healing all that were oppressed of the devil; for God was with him.

It can never be the case that Almighty God is with you and there's nothing to show for it. Are rivers of living water flowing from within you? How many people have you refreshed so far? Are you a blessing to your family, your church, your workplace, your neighborhood, your city, your nation, your generation, or your world? Or a curse or liability to them? As you desire to bless others more and more, declare confidently:

BECAUSE I BELIEVE IN CHRIST JESUS, RIVERS OF LIVING WATER FLOW FROM WITHIN ME!

I shall leave an inheritance for my children's children

A good person leaves an inheritance for their children's children, but a sinner's wealth is stored up for the righteous.

Proverbs 13:22, NIV

Are you a good person? If yes, then by the grace of God you can declare that you shall leave an inheritance, not only for your children, but for your children's children too.

You can make this declaration with confidence if you have filed many prayers in heaven on behalf of your children, and you have been a good role model for them. The good example you have set and the wise advice you have given will be remembered and quoted from generation to generation.

In addition, whatever property you leave to them should have been honestly acquired. Ill-gotten gains seldom reach to the third generation: the general experience of men shows this to be true, and even the heathens know this.

To amass wealth just for personal pleasure is to invite the wrath of God and also to labour for the righteous, who will inherit your riches and use them to take care of the poor and needy and to further God's Kingdom (*Luke 12:16-21*).

The inheritance you leave behind does not refer only to material possessions but to anything of worth, such as your values or your faith. Once this legacy is planted in the hearts of your children, it can be bequeathed to your children's children.

What valuable possessions are you planning to leave for your children's children? Material stuff is not bad, but spiritual assets are of greater value: such as our faith in God, our reverential fear of Him, and our love for our fellowmen. You can also leave a legacy of loving family relationships and godly values of integrity, excellence, hard work, discipline, faith, growth and fruitfulness. Even if you do not yet have children of your own or you only have spiritual children, you must consider the legacy you are going to leave for them.

My Dad worked hard to provide us with material comforts, but what was more important was his spiritual legacy. He left us with this message from *1 Corinthians 11:1*: "Be ye followers of me, even as I also am of Christ." This is also the legacy I intend to leave for my children, apart from whatever material possessions God might bless me with.

To leave a good legacy behind you, you need to:

- Live an exemplary Christian life;
- Sow into the work of God;
- Bless others with the things God has blessed you with;
- Be a good steward in using the gifts God has given you;
- Formulate a strategic plan to generate wealth and not count on just a 9 to 5 job;
- Invest wisely.

These steps will help you to leave a rich inheritance, both spiritually and materially, like Abraham, Isaac and Jacob did. Such a legacy glorifies the God we serve. We must do our best not to end up like the prophet who died indebted, leaving his wife and children at the mercy of his creditors (*2 Kings 4:1-7*).

As you allow the Spirit to empower and lead you to produce wealth and leave a godly example, you can declare confidently:

I SHALL LEAVE AN INHERITANCE FOR MY CHILDREN'S CHILDREN!

Because God has forgiven me, I forgive others too

And be ye kind one to another, tenderhearted, forgiving one another, even as God for Christ's sake hath forgiven you.

Ephesians 4:32

And forgive us our debts, as we forgive our debtors.

Matthew 6:12

The story is told of a leader who had an arch enemy. When the leader came to power in his country, he gave his enemy a key position in his government, to everyone's surprise. This certainly is not what most people would have done, but it was a wise move: he turned his enemy into his staunch supporter.

We are social beings. As long as we are on earth, we need to relate with one another. As we interact with others, it will not always be smooth sailing. Misunderstandings and conflicts will inevitably arise; and, when these set in and relationships turn sour, it is easy to bear grudges.

It can be difficult to forgive someone who has hurt you deeply. Even when people say they have forgiven the offender, most often they have not really forgiven; the forgiveness might only be from their lips, but the heart is not involved.

Some might say, "I forgive you but I will never forget what you did." It is true that forgiving someone who betrayed your trust does not warrant a restoration of that trust in the next minute. Some will even go so far as to say, "Forgive you? Over my dead body!" or words to that effect. But God, on His part, both forgives and forgets completely:

> As far as the east is from the west, so far has He removed our transgressions from us.
>
> *Psalm 103:12, NKJV*

To forgive is to show mercy; it is to say that we no longer have the intention to punish the person who has wronged us. It means no longer holding onto any hard feelings we may have towards the offender. It is not a sign of weakness, but rather it shows our maturity in the ways of God. Our God is our perfect example of forgiveness:

> But God demonstrates His own love toward us, in that while we were still sinners, Christ died for us.
>
> *Romans 5:8, NKJV*

> God was reconciling the world to himself in Christ, not counting people's sins against them. And he has committed to us the message of reconciliation.
>
> *2 Corinthians 5:19, NIV*

Joseph is another good example of someone who forgave much. Many of us would have thought of taking revenge on our siblings if they had sold us into slavery, but Joseph did not. He refused to pay back evil for evil. When God promoted him to be governor of Egypt, his brothers thought he would take revenge on them, since he was in a position of power over them. But instead he assured them:

> Now therefore be not grieved, nor angry with yourselves, that ye sold me hither: for God did send me before you to preserve life.
>
> *Genesis 45:5*

Joseph understood that vengeance belongs to the Lord (*Proverbs 20:22; Romans 12:19*) and that, though his enemies might intend evil against him, God would turn it around for his good and the good of those very same enemies:

> "But as for you, you meant evil against me; but God meant it for good, in order to bring it about as it is this day, to save many people alive. Now therefore, do not be afraid; I will provide for you and your little ones." And he comforted them and spoke kindly to them.
>
> *Genesis 50:20-21, NKJV*

God did not wait for us to come to Him before forgiving us. He forgave us when we were unlovable. He was propelled by His unconditional love for us. Because God forgave us, He expects us to follow in His footsteps. To refuse to forgive is to disobey Him (*Ephesians 4:32*). It is to choose to carry poison in our hearts which will destroy us (*Proverbs 14:30, 17:22*). When we refuse to forgive, we stop God from forgiving us and we block His blessings and answers to our prayers:

> "Therefore I say to you, whatever things you ask when you pray, believe that you receive them, and you will have them. And whenever you stand praying, if you have anything against anyone, forgive him, that your Father in heaven may also forgive you your trespasses. But if you do not forgive, neither will your Father in heaven forgive your trespasses."
>
> *Mark 11:24-26, NKJV*

It is important to note that God places greater importance on our relationships with people than our service or sacrifices to Him (*Matthew 5:23-24*). Our treatment of our fellowmen reflects the way we treat God. To treat our fellowmen well is to treat God well (*Matthew 25:34-45*).

God will never ask us to do anything we are unable to do or anything that will not benefit us. To obey Him and follow His example of forgiveness we need to:

- Be filled with His love through faith in Jesus Christ;
- Prayerfully ask Him for grace to forgive;
- Forgive from the heart;
- Forget the offence;
- Forget about taking revenge, but let God avenge us where necessary (*Romans 12:19*).

How we ask for or release forgiveness is equally important. To show we are really sorry, we can say, "I'm sorry, please forgive me." To show we have really forgiven someone, we need to say something like: "It's alright, you are forgiven." It does not help to say hastily, "Ok, I'm sorry..." and then add words to justify ourselves; or to say, "I forgive you but..." and add other words that show we have not wholeheartedly forgiven the offender.

At times, seeking forgiveness might require restitution. If you have stolen from others, it is better to return all the stolen goods to their rightful owners and not simply say "I'm sorry" to these people. This speaks of genuine repentance, as was the case with Zacchaeus (*Luke 19:8*).

You also need wisdom when dealing with sensitive issues. If you have cheated on your spouse, you should certainly seek God's forgiveness, but it might rather complicate matters if you were to disclose your infidelity to him or her, especially if your spouse is unlikely to handle such a disclosure well.

Once forgiveness is given or received sincerely, we need to claim our forgiveness by faith and not allow the enemy to steal our joy. With this in mind, you can declare with confidence:

BECAUSE GOD HAS FORGIVEN ME, I FORGIVE OTHERS TOO!

As I behold Jesus more and more, I move from glory to glory

But we all, with open face beholding as in a glass the glory of the Lord, are changed into the same image from glory to glory, even as by the Spirit of the Lord.

2 Corinthians 3:18

An amazing change occurs in everyone who has spent time with Jesus. It was said of Peter and John that even the Jewish leaders sat up and took notice of them:

> When they saw the courage of Peter and John and realized that they were unschooled, ordinary men, they were astonished and they took note that these men had been with Jesus.
>
> *Acts 4:13, NIV*

Spending time with the Lord in His Word and in prayer is like looking at oneself in a mirror. Mirrors used by the Jews, Greeks and Romans in ancient times were made of highly polished metal. So, it often happened—especially in strong light—that one's face would be greatly illuminated by the reflected light. Similarly, by earnestly contemplating the Gospel of Jesus and believing on Him who is its Author, the soul becomes illuminated with His divine splendour.

This mirror of the Gospel reflects to the believer the image of Him whose perfections it exhibits; and thus we see the glorious form after which our minds are to be fashioned.

114

Then, by believing and receiving the influence of His Spirit, our form is changed into what we behold: the image of God that we had lost by our fall and that has now been recovered and restored by Jesus to us. It is God's face shining upon us— that is, His approbation of us through Christ—that causes us to be transformed into His Divine image.

The Jews were unable to look on the face of Moses, the mediator of the old covenant, and so he was obliged to veil it (*Exodus 34:29-35*). But we Christians with uncovered faces can behold, as clearly as we can see our own face in a mirror, the glorious promises and privileges of the Gospel of Christ. And, as we contemplate and anticipate them with desire and hope, and apprehend them by faith, we move from the glory represented there to the enjoyment of what is represented: the righteousness and true holiness of the God of glory. So, by the energy of that Spirit of Christ which gives life and being to all the promises in the Gospel, we are made partakers of the Divine nature and escape all the corruption in the world.

The light you reflect today depends on the light you have received as you look at Jesus. The greater the light you reflect, the more God is glorified. The more God is glorified, the more you are blessed. Therefore, decide to behold the glory of Christ continuously, that you may move from glory to glory. Stop looking at your problems, limitations, circumstances, weaknesses and failures. You become what you look at.

God's design for you is that your life gets better every day. Today should be better than yesterday because you are beholding Christ, as in a mirror. What matters is what God's Word says about you. Therefore, know your identity in Christ and confess it boldly, declaring with confidence:

AS I BEHOLD JESUS MORE AND MORE, I MOVE FROM GLORY TO GLORY!

Because I walk in love and love never fails, I will never fail

Love never fails. But where there are prophecies, they will cease; where there are tongues, they will be stilled; where there is knowledge, it will pass away.

1 Corinthians 13:8, NIV

What is love from God's perspective... this love that never fails? Why does it not fail? How can I walk in this type of love so that I never fail?

This "God kind" of love can be defined as *taking great care for the welfare of others.* Love is a chief attribute of God. *1 John 4:16* tells us that "God is love; and he that dwelleth in love dwelleth in God, and God in him." The length and breadth and height and depth of God's love are beyond comprehension, for they are infinite (*Ephesians 3:18-19*).

Among the three manifestations of the Godhead, love is unutterably full, perfect and blissful. Towards the holy angels and Christians, God's love is infinite fatherly care and affection. Towards sinners, it is immeasurable compassion.

Love is shown in all of God's works and ways and dictated in His holy law, but it is most signally displayed in the Gospel:

For God so loved the world that He gave His only begotten Son, that whoever believes in Him should not perish but have everlasting life.

John 3:16, NKJV

This is love: not that we loved God, but that he loved us
and sent his Son as an atoning sacrifice for our sins.

1 John 4:10, NIV

When we have this kind of love in us, it would make us delight
in God and obey Him supremely, with all our heart and soul,
and in practical ways love all according to their character—the
good with fellowship of soul, and the evil with Christ-like
benevolence. Such a love would meet and fulfill all the ends of
the law (*Romans 13:8-10*). Without it, none can enter heaven;
and, as the affections of every unregenerate heart are all
mixed with sin—being given to forbidden objects or selfishly
and unduly given to objects not forbidden—we must be "born
again" in order to see God (*John 3:3; 1 John 4:7, 19, 5:4*).

The Greeks call this kind of love *agápe (ἀγάπη agápē)*,
which means "love in a spiritual sense". It refers to true
unconditional love, rather than the attraction suggested by
éros (romantic love).

Agápe is selfless; it gives and expects nothing in return. It
is the word used for "love" in *1 Corinthians 13*, commonly
known as the "love chapter", and is described there and
throughout the New Testament as sacrificial and spiritual
love. Whether the love given is returned or not, the person
continues to love (even without any self-benefit).

Agápe was also used in ancient texts to denote feelings for
one's children and for a spouse, and it was sometimes used to
refer to a love feast too. It can also be described as the feeling
of being content or holding another in high regard. *Agápe* is
used by Christians to express the unconditional love of God.

Agápe is not to be confused with other kinds of love, such
as *éros, philia, storge, ludus, pragma* or *philausia*. *Éros*
(ἔρως *érōs*) is passionate love with sensual desire: romantic
emotion without the balance of logic. It is "love at first sight".

The modern Greek word *erotas* means "intimate love"; however, *éros* does not have to be sexual in nature; it can also be interpreted as a love that is more than *philia* (the love one would have for a family member or friend). It can also apply to dating relationships as well as marriage.

Philia (φιλία philía) is "mental" love. It means friendship or affectionate regard in both ancient and modern Greek. It is a dispassionate, virtuous love that includes loyalty to friends, family and community.

Storge (στοργή storgē) means "affection" in both ancient and modern Greek. It is a natural affection, like that felt by parents for their offspring. It can also mean mere acceptance, or putting up with a situation, as in "loving" a tyrant.

Ludus, or playful love, refers to the affection between children or young lovers. We have all had a taste of it, in the "flirting and teasing" early stages of a relationship. But we also live out our *ludus* when we sit around, bantering and laughing with friends.

The English equivalent of this might be what we call "platonic love": not involving sexual relations but only friendship or affection between people who might otherwise be expected to be physically attracted to each other.

Pragma, or longstanding love, refers to the deep understanding that develops between long-married couples. *Pragma* is about making compromises and exercising patience and tolerance to make a relationship work. With the high rate of divorce today, it might help if more couples could bring a serious dose of *pragma* into their marriages.

Philautia refers to love of the self. The clever Greeks realized there were two types: an unhealthy variety associated with narcissism, where one becomes self-obsessed and focused on personal fame and fortune; and a healthier version that enhances one's wider capacity to love.

Of all the kinds of love we have looked at, the one that clearly stands out as the love that never fails is *agápe*—the God kind of love. It never fails because God never fails. Because God is love. If you long to see victory in your life and not failure, decide today to love God and your fellowmen.

From God's point of view, love is a decision. Love is action. Because you love and you sow seeds of love, the result is a harvest of success every day: for what we sow, we reap. If you are good to others, God will ensure that others will also show you favour; and that is success:

> Give, and it shall be given unto you; good measure, pressed down, and shaken together, and running over, shall men give into your bosom. For with the same measure that ye mete withal it shall be measured to you again.
>
> *Luke 6:38*

It is possible to give without loving, but you cannot love without giving. The Good Samaritan is another example of love in action; he gave of his time and resources and was complimented by the Lord (*Luke 10:30-35*).

We will reap in this life and in the life to come. At the end of our time on earth, it is our acts of love that will count for eternity (*Matthew 25:31-46*). We don't try to show love to merit heaven but because we are of heaven—if Christ Jesus is our Lord and God!

Ask God for opportunities to show love, and you will be a winner in this life and in the life to come. *1 John 3:18* says, "My little children, let us not love in word, neither in tongue; but in deed and in truth." As you step out to love in deed and in truth, declare with confidence:

BECAUSE I WALK IN LOVE AND LOVE NEVER FAILS, I WILL NEVER FAIL!

In Jesus' Name, I am unshakable, unsinkable, indestructible and unstoppable

And he arose, and rebuked the wind, and said unto the sea, Peace, be still. And the wind ceased, and there was a great calm.

Mark 4:39

In the midst of a storm, Jesus was sleeping soundly. No matter how rough the sea was, He was calm. Facing the multitudes, He did not panic; He knew what to do (*John 6:1-6*). Faced with the dead, Jesus did not panic; He simply gave the word and Lazarus came back to life (*John 11:43*). No matter what the challenge was, He kept calm. He was unshakable.

Nothing and nobody could shake Jesus—because He is the Rock of Ages. If He is living in you, you are unshakable. Instead of people and circumstances shaking you, you have got what it takes to shake them. The Bible tells us:

God has not given us a spirit of fear, but of power and of love and of a sound mind.

2 Timothy 1:7, NKJV

If something terrorizes you, it is because you have allowed it. No matter what mountain is standing before you now, refuse to let it intimidate you. Keep calm and speak to it. Declare victory over it as the Holy Spirit leads you. Be it bills, declare that they shall be paid in Jesus' Name. Be it sickness, declare that you are healed in Jesus' Name. If it is a family or work-related problem, declare that it is solved in Jesus' Name.

While the disciples were in the boat, the storm almost sank them (*Mark 4:37*). *Almost...* but not quite. Because Jesus is unsinkable. What is that thing or person who is trying to sink you? Do not allow the Devil to sink you in a pit of despair, no matter how many times you might have failed. Remember: *winners never quit and quitters never win.* Because Jesus is unsinkable and you belong to Him, you are unsinkable too. As long as Jesus is in your boat, you are unsinkable.

> And when Jesus had cried out with a loud voice, He said, "Father, 'into Your hands I commit My spirit.'" Having said this, He breathed His last.
>
> *Luke 23:46, NKJV*

The Jewish leaders nailed Jesus to the cross, thinking they could destroy Him. But He is indestructible; He simply handed His Spirit over into His Father's hand. What is that thing or person who is trying to destroy you, either directly or indirectly? Declare with faith and boldness: "Because I belong to Jesus, I am indestructible in Jesus' Name."

> And when they looked, they saw that the stone was rolled away: for it was very great.
>
> *Mark 16:4*

Then they laid Him in a tomb and sealed His tomb as tightly as possible. But the stone was rolled away, because He is unstoppable. What is that thing or person who is trying to stop you from fulfilling your dream or your destiny? Declare confidently: "Because I belong to Jesus, I am unstoppable."

No matter who or what you are facing now, declare boldly:

IN JESUS' NAME, I AM UNSHAKABLE, UNSINKABLE, INDESTRUCTIBLE AND UNSTOPPABLE!

I am saved to serve

Jesus called them together and said, "Among the heathen, kings are tyrants and each minor official lords it over those beneath him. But among you it is quite different. Anyone wanting to be a leader among you must be your servant. And if you want to be right at the top, you must serve like a slave.

"Your attitude must be like my own, for I, the Messiah, did not come to be served, but to serve, and to give my life as a ransom for many."

Matthew 20:25-28, TLB

Everyone is a leader in one way or another. Worldly leadership has things upside down. In the world, to lead is to exercise authority, to dominate. In God's Kingdom, the opposite is true. In God's Kingdom, to lead is to serve.

In God's Kingdom, service is a privilege. Before we came into this world, God had already foreordained good works specifically for each one of us to do:

> For we are his workmanship, created in Christ Jesus unto good works, which God hath before ordained that we should walk in them.
>
> *Ephesians 2:10*

Jeremiah, for example, was foreordained to be a prophet. This is what God told him:

> "Before I formed you in the womb I knew you; before you were born I sanctified you; I ordained you a prophet to the nations."
>
> *Jeremiah 1:5, NKJV*

When we serve, we are showing our love for our Lord and our appreciation for what He has done for us:

> But you are a chosen generation, a royal priesthood, a holy nation, His own special people, that you may proclaim the praises of Him who called you out of darkness into His marvelous light.
>
> *1 Peter 2:9, NKJV*

You are saved to serve. There are no spectators in the House of God. But what does serving involve? Why and how are we to go about it? To serve is to be a servant to somebody. It means to perform duties; to attend to someone or work for someone. Jesus is our perfect example of service: He "did not come to be served, but to serve, and to give His life a ransom for many" (*Matthew 20:28, NKJV*). Before He went to the cross, He demonstrated the extent to which we are to lay down our lives for others:

> Ye call me Master and Lord: and ye say well; for so I am. If I then, your Lord and Master, have washed your feet; ye also ought to wash one another's feet.
>
> For I have given you an example, that ye should do as I have done to you. Verily, verily, I say unto you, the servant is not greater than his lord; neither he that is sent greater than he that sent him. If ye know these things, happy are ye if ye do them.
>
> *John 13:13-17*

Sad to say, we often find more spectators than servants in the House of God. Many prefer to be served rather than to serve. Someone has said that the church today is like a football stadium. Only a few are involved in the action, while the majority are spectators. Those in leadership positions rarely consider themselves as servants. Instead, they lord it over the flock. This is not what the Bible teaches.

> To the elders among you, I appeal as a fellow elder and a witness of Christ's sufferings who also will share in the glory to be revealed:
>
> Be shepherds of God's flock that is under your care, watching over them—not because you must, but because you are willing, as God wants you to be; not pursuing dishonest gain, but eager to serve; not lording it over those entrusted to you, but being examples to the flock.
>
> And when the Chief Shepherd appears, you will receive the crown of glory that will never fade away.
>
> *1 Peter 5:1-4, NIV*

The Lordship of Jesus is absent from many so-called churches today. Most are run like business enterprises, with one big "man of God" at the head and the ministerial staff at his service. This is not the way the church is to be run. Jesus alone is the head of the church, and all members in His church are on an equal footing, but with different responsibilities.

It is true that those who assist in providing direction to the church are to be honored; but they are not to be worshiped, as is the case in certain quarters. No matter what position we hold in the church of Jesus Christ, we are all servants—though He chooses to call us His friends.

Our gifts can be an indication of how we can serve Him:

> If your gift is prophesying, then prophesy in accordance with your faith; if it is serving, then serve; if it is teaching, then teach; if it is to encourage, then give encouragement; if it is giving, then give generously; if it is to lead, do it diligently; if it is to show mercy, do it cheerfully.
>
> *Romans 12:6-8, NIV*

We are to look out for opportunities to serve (*Galatians 6:10*). If someone needs a babysitter and we avail ourselves, we are serving Jesus. If we know of people who are in hospital or jail and we visit them, we are serving Jesus. If the poor in our community need financial assistance or food or clothing, and we provide for their needs, that is service too.

> Pure and genuine religion in the sight of God the Father means caring for orphans and widows in their distress and refusing to let the world corrupt you.
>
> *James 1:27, NLT*

No service in the House of God is too big or too small. We each have a role to play, a contribution to make for the whole body of Christ to function well:

> For as the body is one and has many members, but all the members of that one body, being many, are one body, so also is Christ.
>
> *1 Corinthians 12:12, NKJV*

The joy and blessings that flow from serving God are beyond expression. The apostle Paul testified to this when he said:

> I was a constant example to you in helping the poor; for I remembered the words of the Lord Jesus, "It is more blessed to give than to receive."
>
> *Acts 20:35, TLB*

The story is told of a great man of God who was invited to attend an important event. God had used him to do mighty exploits for His Kingdom; so, upon arrival, he headed for the VIP chair, assuming it had been reserved for him. But, to his great surprise, he was ushered to a humbler seat.

Curious to know who was considered more important than him, he kept a close watch on the VIP seat. Soon, he saw an elderly lady being escorted to the seat and, upon inquiry, learnt that she had been praying diligently for him. The great exploits the man of God had accomplished were all thanks to the faithful prayers of this elderly lady!

Speaking of faithfulness, the apostle Paul declared, "it is required that those who have been given a trust must prove faithful" (*1 Corinthians 4:2, NIV*). Faithfulness, excellence, humility, sacrifice and willingness: these should be the hallmarks that characterize those serving in God's Kingdom.

We are to be consistent in serving God. We are not to serve only when it is convenient. We are to give excellent service, giving the best of ourselves for the glory of the Lord:

> Therefore, my beloved brothers and sisters, be steadfast, immovable, always excelling in the work of the Lord [always doing your best and doing more than is needed], being continually aware that your labor [even to the point of exhaustion] in the Lord is not futile nor wasted.
>
> *1 Corinthians 15:58, AMP*

We are to serve even when no one is watching, serving with integrity and not for the sake of gain. We are to serve wholeheartedly at all times, knowing that we are serving the King of Kings and the Lord of Lords:

> Whatever you do, work at it with all your heart, as working for the Lord, not for human masters, since you know that you will receive an inheritance from the Lord as a reward. It is the Lord Christ you are serving.
>
> *Colossians 3:23-24, NIV*

Sacrificial service means going out of our way to see our Lord served. It might require dusting the church benches very early on a Sunday morning or giving sacrificially to missions. Also, we should not expect to be applauded at all times. Often, all that we do will go unnoticed, unappreciated and unrewarded. But we should still continue to serve humbly and joyfully. Speaking about joyful service in spite of all odds, the prophet

Habakkuk averred that, although his labor might go totally unrewarded, "Yet I will rejoice in the Lord, I will joy in the God of my salvation" (*Habakkuk 3:17-18*).

Another good example of humble and willing service is Mary, who offered herself as an instrument in God's hand for Him to use. When the angel Gabriel appeared to her, her response was, "I am the Lord's servant, and I am willing to do whatever he wants" (*Luke 1:38, TLB*).

Finally, Christ Himself is our greatest example of sacrificial, humble, faithful, excellent and willing service:

> Who, being in very nature God, did not consider equality with God something to be used to his own advantage; rather, he made himself nothing by taking the very nature of a servant, being made in human likeness. And being found in appearance as a man, he humbled himself by becoming obedient to death—even death on a cross!
>
> Therefore God exalted him to the highest place and gave him the name that is above every name, that at the name of Jesus every knee should bow, in heaven and on earth and under the earth, and every tongue acknowledge that Jesus Christ is Lord, to the glory of God the Father.
>
> *Philippians 2:6-11, NIV*

The key to blessings and promotion from God is dedicated service. Hard work always pays. Those who are diligent in serving will stand before kings (*Proverbs 22:29*). They that serve well with the little they have will be given more opportunities to serve (*Matthew 25:21*).

What will Jesus say to you when He returns? Will He say, "Well done, good and faithful servant"? If the answer is yes, praise the Lord. If no, it's not too late to start serving. Declare:

I AM SAVED TO SERVE!

Because I love God and am called according to His purpose, all things work together for my good and not my destruction

And we know that all things work together for good to them that love God, to them who are the called according to his purpose.

Romans 8:28

"All things" means *all things*. Even when we fail colossally, God has something good for us to learn from our failures. Even when you are broke or sick or mistreated or deceived, or when you lose a job or a loved one, or when you fail an exam, or when you are misunderstood or disappointed... all these things are working for your good! Certainly, they are difficult to accept. But nothing that happens to us takes God by surprise. There are no "accidents" with God:

> For I know the plans I have for you," declares the Lord, "plans to prosper you and not to harm you, plans to give you hope and a future.
>
> *Jeremiah 29:11, NIV*

Paul tells us, "In everything give thanks: for this is the will of God in Christ Jesus concerning you" (*1 Thessalonians 5:18*).

We give thanks, not because the bad things are nice, but because we know God is in control. Giving thanks when things go wrong is a demonstration of our faith.

My wife and I had a matter to sort out with the National Social Insurance Fund in our country. The matter took a long time to solve, and all our efforts to follow up on it proved to be fruitless. Reminding ourselves that all things work together for our good, we decided that we were going to stop asking God to intervene as far as this problem was concerned. We decided to change gears, so to speak.

Yes, God inhabits the praises of His people. Like Paul and Silas in prison, we began to praise God for the situation, giving Him thanks in advance for handling the matter. Before long, it was resolved and we had more reasons to rejoice in God. Truly, because you love God and are called according to His purposes, all things will certainly work together for your good, and you will have reason to glorify God more and more.

Joseph is a prime testimony to the truth of *Romans 8:28*. When he was dumped into a pit by his brothers, all was going well for his good. When his brothers sold him as a slave and he was taken to Egypt, all was working for his good. When he was falsely accused by Potiphar's wife, all was working for his good. When he was thrown into jail, it was all for his good. When he was forgotten in jail by someone who could have helped him, all was working for his good. All of that led finally to his promotion from prison to palace (*Genesis 37, 39-41*).

There's a palace waiting for you too. Only cooperate with God instead of complaining, and He will take you there in the fullness of time. Declare with confidence today:

BECAUSE I LOVE GOD AND AM CALLED ACCORDING TO HIS PURPOSE, ALL THINGS WORK TOGETHER FOR MY GOOD AND NOT MY DESTRUCTION, IN THE NAME OF JESUS!

Because God's hand is upon me, expansion is my portion

Enlarge the place of thy tent, and let them stretch forth the curtains of thine habitations: spare not, lengthen thy cords, and strengthen thy stakes;

For thou shalt break forth on the right hand and on the left; and thy seed shall inherit the Gentiles, and make the desolate cities to be inhabited.

Isaiah 54:2-3

Long before it happened, the prophet Isaiah announced the conversion of the Gentiles. The message above was addressed to the Jews: "thy seed shall inherit the Gentiles"; that is, Israel's spiritual seed, the Church, would bring the Gentiles to Christ. "On the right hand and on the left" refers to the multitudes who would come from all over the world.

Therefore, Israel—or her seed, the Church—is to enlarge her tent. The allusion here is to the tabernacle, which has to be enlarged to accommodate the new crowds of worshippers: the stakes are to be driven deep and firm, and the cords lengthened and tightened, that the sides of the tent may be able to support the pressure of the multitudes within it.

When God speaks of expansion, it is in relation to what He sees coming. He predicted expansion through Isaiah, and we are seeing its fulfilment. The Church started small at Pentecost, but it will not end small. The population of nominal Christians in the world today is believed to be about two billion.

God's message is addressed to the Church Universal, but it equally concerns you as a member of the body of Christ. Our God is a big God. Too often we limit Him in our thoughts, and this is reflected in our actions. It is time for you to consider expansion in every area of your life. Crave for more of God, more of the manifestation of His power and gifts in you. God always responds to our hunger (*Matthew 5:6*). Crave for the salvation of more souls. God has promised us:

> "Ask of me, and I shall give thee the heathen for thine inheritance, and the uttermost parts of the earth for thy possession."
>
> *Psalm 2:8*

God wants a full house of true worshipers (*John 4:23-24, Luke 14:23*). He wants us to depopulate Hell and populate Heaven. Crave for more committed disciples of Jesus. For God to bring expansion, I have a key role to play. As I crave and take the necessary measures, expansion will come.

Expansion brings greater honour to our God. When Jesus entered Jerusalem with pomp, the whole city shook. Those who did not know Jesus heard about Him that day. Those who tried to silence the disciples were told that God is able to raise stones to praise Him (*Luke 19:37-40*).

Paul tells us: "all of creation is waiting, yearning for the time when the children of God will be revealed (*Romans 8:19, TV*). Children of God are solution providers. We must dream big to see expansion so that we can bring hope to the hopeless, provide food for the hungry and housing for the homeless, clothe the naked, educate the illiterate and do so much more.

The world is big, with big needs. Unless we expand, we cannot make a big difference. This is not to say our little acts of kindness are not appreciated by God (*Matthew 10:42*), but so much more needs to be done.

Think about an area where we are not expanding. Is it in the field of evangelism, discipleship, finances, technology, sports, music, academics or the sciences? Where do you wish to see growth that will bring maximum glory to God? Identify that area and begin to believe God for expansion.

Do not allow people or circumstances to negate your faith. Jesus said, "If you can believe, all things are possible to him who believes" (*Mark 9:23, NKJV*). Whatever will happen to us in reality must first happen in our minds. If we can see it in our minds, then we can see it in reality. Here are some steps you can take to expand your faith and see greater results:

- Spend more time in the Word
- Pray more
- Associate with people who are growing in their faith
- Make use of faith-building materials like books and videos

As expansion comes, remain humble and give God the glory. Most people seek God for expansion but, when it comes, they easily forget that it is only because of God that they have what they have. They become ungrateful. They become proud and unapproachable, greedy and wicked. Do not be like them.

Of the ten lepers Jesus healed (*Luke 17:12-19*), only one returned to thank Him; and, sadly enough, he was a Samaritan and not a Jew. Do we, as God's children, remember to thank Him for all He has done for us? Or are we like many so-called Christians who might not be as grateful to God as they ought to?

God might withhold expansion from us if it will destroy us —for example, if it will cause us to turn away from Him or become proud—or if we cannot manage the little He has given us (*Luke 16:10-12*). But, where our desire is to bless others and glorify Him, He *will* grant us expansion. Declare confidently:

BECAUSE GOD'S HAND IS UPON ME, EXPANSION IS MY PORTION!

Because I am a king, where my word is, there is power

Where the word of a king is, there is power; and who may say to him, "What are you doing?"

Ecclesiastes 8:4, NKJV

And hath made us kings and priests unto God and his Father; to him be glory and dominion for ever and ever.

Revelation 1:6

If you are part of God's kingdom, you are a priest and a king. Jesus is our High Priest and King of kings. These are two different roles: priests intercede; kings rule. Today our focus is on our kingly role.

As kings in God's kingdom, we were born to dominate over His creation. But we are not to rule like worldly kings. We are not to oppress our fellow human beings.

We rule, not only over God's creation, but over evil forces too. Though Jesus disarmed and disgraced principalities and powers on the cross (*Colossians 2:15*), the war is not over. The enemy is not yet crushed. He is still alive, and he operates through lies. Jesus, however, assures us, "you shall know the truth, and the truth shall make you free" (*John 8:32, NKJV*).

The truth is that you are a king, even if you don't feel like one. You are a godly king; that is why *Psalm 82:6* says, "I have said, Ye are gods; and all of you are children of the most High."

As a king, you need to learn how to comport yourself with dignity, equanimity and authority. Your authority lies in your mouth. Your word is you. Anyone who disrespects the word of the king is disrespecting the king. Because you are a king, where your word is, there is power.

Psalm 33:6 tells us, "By the word of the LORD were the heavens made" and, in Genesis chapter 1, we see how God created the world by His spoken word. God Himself has exalted His word above His name; in *Psalm 138:2,* the psalmist declared, "thou hast magnified thy word above all thy name".

Because you are God's offspring, you also release power when you speak; your words produce results! Jesus understood this—which was why, when He spoke to the fig tree and the storm, they had to obey Him (*Mark 11:13-14, 20; Luke 8:23-24*). We can do likewise, for He Himself has said we can move mountains by our words:

> "Truly I tell you, if you have faith as small as a mustard seed, you can say to this mountain, 'Move from here to there,' and it will move. Nothing will be impossible for you."
>
> *Matthew 17:20, NIV*

Mountains speak of the challenges before you. Challenges are opportunities to exercise your kingly authority. Speak in faith and the mountain, which is your difficulty, will be removed.

Where your word is, there is power to save, heal, deliver and bless. Speak healing to that body, to that relationship, to that child, to that spouse, to that business, to that bank account... and wait to see miraculous results!

Step out in faith and begin to declare confidently:

BECAUSE I AM A KING IN GOD'S KINGDOM, WHERE MY WORD IS, THERE IS POWER!

Because I am righteous, I am as bold as a lion

The wicked flee when no one pursues, but the righteous are bold as a lion.

Proverbs 28:1, NKJV

To be righteous is to do what is morally right, obeying God's commands. It is to be in right standing with God. The righteous are those who have placed their faith in Jesus as their Lord and God. They believe Jesus died for their sins and rose again (*Romans 10:9*). To be right with God brings boldness because:

- Jesus has washed away our sins
- God is on our side
- The Spirit of God strengthens us from the inside
- We know our identity in Christ

The righteous are not only bold, they are bold *as a lion*. The lion is known to be strong, confident and alert; so are the righteous. Like a lion, they go out boldly—not to destroy their fellowmen—but to terrorize the kingdom of darkness and undertake great exploits in life.

Jesus is "the Lion of the tribe of Judah" (*Revelation 5:5*). If Jesus lives in you, the real lion—the Lion of the tribe of Judah—lives in you. This is why *1 John 4:4* tells us, "greater is he [Jesus] that is in you [the believer], than he [Satan] that is in the world". Ignorance of your identity in Christ will expose you to attacks and trouble from the kingdom of darkness, because "your enemy the devil prowls around like a roaring lion looking for someone to devour" (*1 Peter 5:8, NIV*).

The devil is not a lion; he just prowls around like one. The real Lion lives in you, if you have Christ. If Christ lives in you, you are righteous, and you are called to be as bold as a lion.

Are you being threatened by anybody or any situation? Is there fear in your heart—of the dark, of demons, of witchcraft, of financial disasters or of some other calamity? If yes, you can exercise your authority over every contrary spirit, because the Lion of the tribe of Judah is living in you. Jesus declared:

> Behold, I give unto you power to tread on serpents and scorpions, and over all the power of the enemy: and nothing shall by any means hurt you.
>
> *Luke 10:19*

The devil plays on our ignorance, and this ignorance can destroy us (*Hosea 4:6*) if we do not know our identity in Christ. But once you know who you are, you can stand up to the challenge. Thanks to his connection with God, David overcame Goliath (*1 Samuel 17:48-51*). No matter how big your Goliath is, you can deal with him as David did.

Without boldness, we can never achieve anything worthwhile in life. So, step out boldly to take territories for Jesus and expand God's kingdom; live out your faith boldly in your home, neighborhood and workplace. As long as we are led by the Spirit of Christ, nothing and no one should intimidate us as we go about spreading the good news of salvation in Christ.

Undertake business ventures with wisdom and boldness, and for God's glory. Failure to make a move for fear of failure is the greatest failure. Let us not allow fear to steal our inheritance, for God has not given us a spirit of fear, but of power and of love and of a sound mind (*2 Timothy 1:7*).

If Christ is your life, you can declare confidently:

BECAUSE I AM RIGHTEOUS, I AM AS BOLD AS A LION

God's plans for me are to prosper me, to give me hope and a future

For I know the plans I have for you," declares the LORD, "plans to prosper you and not to harm you, plans to give you hope and a future."

Jeremiah 29:11, NIV

As long as we live on planet earth, we will face challenges. Jesus tells us, "In the world you will have tribulation"; but then He goes on to assure us, "be of good cheer, I have overcome the world" (*John 16:33, NKJV*). It is very easy, however, to forget His Word in the heat of life's battles.

John the Baptist did not have it easy when he was locked up in jail and Jesus didn't show up to deliver him. John sent his disciples to ask Jesus whether He was the Messiah they were expecting or if they should wait for someone else. Jesus' reply makes it clear that, no matter what we may be going through, God is always in control and never stops performing His miracles (*Luke 7: 18-22*).

Even if nothing seems to be going well for us, it does not mean that God has abandoned us, for He has assured us:

"I WILL NEVER [under any circumstances] DESERT YOU [nor give you up nor leave you without support, nor will I in any degree leave you helpless], nor will I forsake or let you down or relax My hold on you [assuredly not]!"

Hebrews 13:5, AMP

No matter what you may be going through right now, God is working behind the scenes to bring about an end result that will be wholly satisfying for you—even beyond all you could ever imagine or ask for:

> Now to Him who is able to do exceedingly abundantly above all that we ask or think, according to the power that works in us, to Him be glory in the church by Christ Jesus to all generations, forever and ever. Amen.
>
> *Ephesians 3:20-21, NKJV*

Does this mean I can live any way I like and still expect God to fulfill His purposes for me? Far from it! To his own question, "Shall we continue in sin that grace may abound?" Paul emphatically declared, "Certainly not! How shall we who died to sin live any longer in it?" (*Romans 6:1-2, NKJV*)

When we sin willfully, God will punish us. But, if we are making efforts to live right, He will cause His grace to abound in us, so that we are able to do what is right. We strive to live right, not to merit His favour, but because it is for our own good to do so. At the end of the day, where sin abounds, His grace abounds even more (*Romans 5:20*), for He does not treat us according to our sins (*Psalm 103:10*).

Some challenges that come our way may have been caused by sin on our part. We see cases of this in the Old Testament: when the children of Israel sinned against God, He did not hesitate to punish them. But, every time they repented, God forgave them and restored them to Himself.

At other times we might face hardship, not necessarily because of sin or because God willed it but because He allowed it into our lives to try us—as was the case with Job. Job did not suffer because he had sinned but because God allowed Satan to try him (*Job 1:9-12; 2:3-6*). During this period of trial, Job kept his faith. This is what we must do in the midst of trials—

put our faith in God. Our focus must be on Him, not on our challenges. In the end, everything Job had lost was restored to him, and much more—beyond all that he could ever have imagined (*Job 42:10-15*). Job's life story is an inspiring testimony; it tells us that, no matter what we may go through, God's will for our good always prevails in the end.

> And we know that in all things God works for the good of those who love him, who have been called according to his purpose.
>
> *Romans 8:28, NIV*

Life's experiences are like the ingredients that go into making a cake. It would be awful to consume some of them separately, such as raw eggs, butter or flour. It takes a mixture, a blending of these ingredients—all of which are necessary—to come up with a delectable cake. In the same way, God takes all our life experiences, blends everything together, and makes all things beautiful in His own time. He has promised to give us beauty for our ashes (*Isaiah 61:3*). He has also assured us that He will be with us when we go through tough times:

> When you pass through the waters, I will be with you;
> And through the rivers, they shall not overflow you.
> When you walk through the fire, you shall not be burned,
> Nor shall the flame scorch you.
>
> *Isaiah 43:2, NKJV*

No matter what you are going through now or may go through in future, always remain connected to God. And be assured that, though weeping may endure for what seems like a very long night, joy always comes in the morning (*Psalm 30:5*). This is why you can declare with confidence:

GOD'S PLANS FOR ME ARE TO PROSPER ME, TO GIVE ME HOPE AND A FUTURE

I am as strong as a horse because I rejoice in the Lord always

"Do not sorrow, for the joy of the LORD is your strength."

Nehemiah 8:10, NKJV

Rejoice in the Lord always: and again I say, Rejoice.

Philippians 4:4

The JOY of the LORD is our strength. We are commanded to rejoice in Him always because it is great medicine for our souls. It also confuses the devil. It is our master card. When all seems lost, rejoice and sing praises to the Lord—and the demons will quickly disappear.

When Saul was in a bad mood, David would play on his harp, and the joyful music would drive away the evil spirit that was tormenting the king (*1 Samuel 16:23*). When Elisha needed to prophesy at one point, he had to call on a musician before the anointing could flow: "And as the lute was played, the message of the Lord came to Elisha" (*2 Kings 3:15, TLB*).

Such is the power of praise that it has often been said, "to sing praises to God is to pray twice". We are to sing and rejoice in the Lord always, for the joy of the Lord is our strength. But what exactly is the joy of the Lord? How is it our strength?

The kind of joy we are talking about comes from the Holy Spirit. *Galatians 5:22-23* tells us that the fruit of the Spirit is love, *joy*, peace, patience, kindness, goodness, faithfulness, gentleness and self-control.

This joy is a state of contentment in God. It is different from happiness: while happiness depends on circumstances, joy does not depend on what is happening around us. We can be joyful, whether things are working out well or not.

Someone has defined joy as:

Jesus first

Others second

You last

Truly, if you put Jesus first and others before yourself, you will always be contented. *Matthew 16:25* tells us that whoever desires to save his life will lose it, but whoever loses his life for Jesus will find it.

Discouragement is inevitable in life. As God's children, we are not spared from times of discouragement. What matters is not whether discouragements come but what we do when they come. What happened to David while he was living among the Philistines—before he became king of Israel—is a case in point. While David and his men were away from home, the Amalekites came and burned down their city and took away their wives and children:

> Then David and the people who were with him lifted up their voices and wept, until they had no more power to weep.
>
> *1 Samuel 30:4, NKJV*

The men were in such despair that the only thought they had left was to stone David:

> And David was greatly distressed; for the people spake of stoning him, because the soul of all the people was grieved, every man for his sons and for his daughters: but David encouraged himself in the LORD his God.
>
> *1 Samuel 30:6*

David encouraged himself in the LORD his God! It is very easy to get discouraged by challenges, but we must refuse to be overwhelmed by them. David could encourage himself in the Lord because he believed his God would be more than able to see him through—and GOD DID! David knew a God who had been faithful in the past and who would always be faithful; a God who would cause him to see His goodness in the land of the living (*Psalm 27:13*).

Rejoicing in the Lord in the midst of challenges does not mean pretending that those challenges do not exist. It is a question of choosing to focus on God and not on the challenges. It is choosing to celebrate God, even when you don't feel like praising Him.

Psalm 22:3 tells us that God inhabits the praises of His people. When you begin to praise God from your heart, He steps into your situation and releases His strength into your spirit, enabling you to sail through the roughest waters. Paul and Silas experienced this when they were thrown into prison:

> About midnight Paul and Silas were praying and singing hymns to God, and the other prisoners were listening to them. Suddenly there was such a violent earthquake that the foundations of the prison were shaken. At once all the prison doors flew open, and everyone's chains came loose.
>
> *Acts 16:25-26, NIV*

Stop now and praise God like crazy! Our lives are to be filled with praise unto God because that is what we were created for (*Psalm 150*). Knowing this, let us declare with confidence:

I AM AS STRONG AS A HORSE BECAUSE I REJOICE IN THE LORD ALWAYS!

I am blessed beyond the curse

"No curse can be placed on Jacob, and no magic shall be done against him. For now it shall be said of Israel, 'What wonders God has done for them!'"

Numbers 23:23, TLB

And God said to Balaam, "You shall not... curse the people, for they are blessed."

Numbers 22:12, NKJV

Balak, king of Moab, tried to get Balaam to put a curse on the children of Israel so that he could defeat them, but he failed (*Numbers 22:1-24:19*). The prophet could only bless them.

Today and forevermore, all the Balaks who try to put a curse on you will inevitably fail. When they open their mouths to curse you, only blessings will come out, for no one can curse what God has blessed. As long as you belong to God and stay connected to Him, you are blessed beyond the curse of anyone.

No weapon formed against you shall prosper, and every tongue which rises against you in judgment you shall condemn. This is the heritage of the servants of the LORD, and their righteousness is from Me," says the LORD.

Isaiah 54:17, NKJV

No one can touch you. *Psalm 105:15* says that God rebukes kings for our sake. "Touch not mine anointed," He warns, "and do my prophets no harm." Whoever touches you touches God, for you are the apple of His eye (*Deuteronomy 32:10*).

143

If we, as parents, take such good care of our children, how much more does God our Father! The devil comes to steal, kill and destroy; but Jesus is the Good Shepherd who protects us and blesses us with abundant life (*John 10:10-11*).

To be blessed by God is to be uplifted and empowered by Him; to enjoy His favour and prosperity. *Proverbs 10:22* tells us that the blessing of the Lord makes us rich and free from sorrow. He blesses us so that our lives might bring Him glory and we might be a blessing to others. In line with this, God told Abraham:

> "I will make you into a great nation, and I will bless you; I will make your name great, and you will be a blessing. I will bless those who bless you, and whoever curses you I will curse; and all peoples on earth will be blessed through you."
>
> *Genesis 12:2-3, NIV*

The blessing is the enablement, and the blessings flow from the enablement. You might not have a house or a car or much money in your pocket now, but this does not mean you have missed out on your blessing. It is God's *blessing* on you that enables you to call forth the blessings—houses, cars, money, and so forth. More importantly, even if you have none of this world's goods, you are still blessed if you are born again; for *Colossians 1:27* tells us that Christ in us is our hope of a glorious life.

As long as you stay connected to God, no one can stop you from getting to where God has ordained. Only you can stop yourself through ignorance or unbelief (*Numbers 13:26-33; Hosea 4:6*). Because God has blessed you, you are bound to succeed in all your endeavours. Therefore, declare confidently:

I AM BLESSED BEYOND THE CURSE OF ANYONE, IN THE NAME OF JESUS!

Because I trust in the Lord, I shall never be put to shame

"Listen carefully, I am laying in Zion a Stone, a tested Stone, a precious Cornerstone for the [secure] foundation, firmly placed. He who believes [who trusts in, relies on, and adheres to that Stone] will not be disturbed or give way [in sudden panic].

Isaiah 28:16, AMP

"Those who wait for me shall never be ashamed."

Isaiah 49:23, TLB

"Behold, I lay in Zion a stumbling stone and rock of offense, and whoever believes on Him will not be put to shame."

Romans 9:33, NKJV

The above verses are among my favourites in the whole Bible. I can attest to their truth, having experienced it in my own life. Countless times, I have had a need, not knowing where the solution was going to come from; but, as I continued to trust the Lord, He would always show up in time with the solution.

The devil, the enemy of our souls, is always looking for ways to bring mockery and disgrace to the children of God, and he will use every means at his disposal to do this. It can be through close or distant persons. The devil's aim is to cause you to doubt the God you are serving, lose faith in Him, and turn instead to him—the devil—for help.

145

If you are ignorant of the enemy's strategies, it will be very easy to fall for his tricks. Perhaps you have been faithfully giving to God and serving Him; yet, it seems like nothing is working out in your life. Maybe you have been waiting for years for the man or woman of your dreams, but he (or she) has not shown up. To rub salt into the wound, your friends and family have begun mocking at you, as they see all your juniors getting married while you are still single.

Maybe you have been faithfully serving in your workplace for years and you see everyone around you getting promoted—except you. Or perhaps you have been married for years, but the fruit of your womb is not forthcoming. Or you are quite advanced in years but still do not have a house of your own, or your own car, or money in the bank... and meanwhile, all around you, youngsters and unbelievers are getting richer by the day. At such times, it can be very challenging when people start asking you, "Where is your God?" But God says to us, "Do not fret because of those who are evil or be envious of those who do wrong" (*Psalm 37:1, NIV*). He tells us:

> Rest in the LORD, and wait patiently for Him;
> Do not fret because of him who prospers in his way,
> Because of the man who brings wicked schemes to pass.
>
> *Psalm 37:7, NKJV*

God never forgets His own when they cry out to Him every day. The story of Hannah is a good example of His faithfulness. Hannah was childless and, when she could no longer stand the mockery of her rival, Penninah, she decided to pour her heart out to God, to the point of making a vow (*1 Samuel 1:10-11*). God heard her cries and opened her womb. He blessed her with a son who became one of the greatest prophets Israel has ever known, the prophet Samuel.

At the end of the day, Hannah could sing a new song:

"How I rejoice in the Lord!
How he has blessed me!
Now I have an answer for my enemies,
For the Lord has solved my problem.
How I rejoice!"

1 Samuel 2:1, TLB

There is a time for everything under the sun. If Hannah ended up singing a new song, you too will sing a new song when your time comes. And it will come! Our God is always on time: never too late and never too early.

Refrain from saying anything negative. Don't say, "God is not fair." Or, "Why me?" Or, "I am finished." Brush off the self-pity and self-doubt. Brush off the regrets. Wipe off your tears and put on a smile. God is on your side and you are a winner in Christ. You will make it, in Jesus' Name.

Your Samuel will come, and many more blessings besides. What happened to Hannah will also happen to you. All is not lost. As long as you are walking in God's plan, you shall never be put to shame, because His eye is on you. You shall never be put to shame—in your physical, family, professional, social, emotional, financial and ministerial life, in Jesus' Name.

I had a sister who sat for an exam year after year without success. But she never gave up. She was not going to be put to shame. She kept on trying until one year she made it, to the glory of God.

Those who have laughed at you will laugh with you. Those who have ridiculed you will be put to shame. Your problem is God's opportunity to demonstrate the reality of His power. Delay is not denial. Simply declare with confidence every day:

BECAUSE I TRUST IN THE LORD, I SHALL NEVER BE PUT TO SHAME!

I am blessed for life

Blessed be the God and Father of our Lord Jesus Christ, who hath blessed us with all spiritual blessings in heavenly places in Christ.

Ephesians 1:3

For the gifts and the calling of God are irrevocable.

Romans 11:29, NKJV

As long as you are in Christ, you are blessed for life; and the greatest of these blessings given to you are God's everlasting heavenly blessings, which include forgiveness of sins, peace and joy, adoption as His child, and eternal life.

As we celebrate and praise God for our spiritual blessings, we will also see a physical manifestation of His blessings. When Paul and Silas were in jail, they prayed and praised God for the privilege of being part of His Kingdom and end-time army; and that time of praise in prison led to their deliverance and the salvation of the jailer (*Acts 16:25–40*).

We don't need to *feel* blessed to *be* blessed. The real blessing is not what we see but what is unseen. Our unseen blessing is what is contained in God's Word. To discover what we really possess, we must spend time searching the Scriptures, as the Bereans did (*Acts 17:11*). The better you understand something, the more you will enjoy it. The more you study God's Word, the more reasons you have to praise Him.

As we go through life, challenges will come our way. You might be growing old, and no spouse is available. You might be married but have been childless a long time. You might be jobless, tormented by an illness, or struggling with poverty.

Whatever tricks that life or the devil tries to play on you, you need to declare in faith that you *are* blessed for life. Say it now! Don't say it only when you have money in your pocket or when you feel blessed. Say it whether you feel it or not. The blessings are not just for today and tomorrow. They are yours *for life!*

Though this might be a controversial topic to some, it is important to remind ourselves that, if we are truly saved today, we are saved *for life*. Our salvation does not depend upon our performance (*Ephesians 2:8-9*). We don't work with God to be saved, but because we *are* saved. This, however, is not a passport for us to live our lives "any old how". As it says in *2 Peter 1:3*, God's divine power has already given us everything we need to live a godly life. Those who claim to be blessed for life and continue in sin are deceiving themselves. The Scriptures clearly say that "God is not mocked; for whatever a man sows, that he will also reap" (*Galatians 6:7, NKJV*).

God has given us the greatest blessing of all, which is Christ. If God has given us Christ, nothing else is too big for Him to give us. As *Romans 8:32* says, if God did not spare His own Son but gave Him up for us all, how shall He not also freely give us all things? Every time you think of this, it is a fresh opportunity for you to appreciate God. In fact, Paul in *Ephesians 1:3* exhorts us to praise God for blessing us with all spiritual blessings in Christ. When we bless God, we open the door for more blessings to come our way (*Psalm 50:23*).

Help someone else get connected to Christ today, so that we can all declare we are blessed for life, for God's glory. And, no matter how you are feeling or what you are going through right now, continue to declare boldly:

I AM BLESSED FOR LIFE, IN THE NAME OF JESUS!

Because I belong to Jesus, His blood speaks better things on my behalf

And to Jesus the mediator of the new covenant, and to the blood of sprinkling, that speaketh better things than that of Abel.

Hebrews 12:24

To say that the blood of Jesus speaks better things on our behalf is to say, together with Paul, that there is now no condemnation for those who are in Christ Jesus (*Romans 8:1*). If you have placed your faith in the finished work of Christ on the cross on your behalf, then you must rid yourself of all condemnation from a guilty conscience. For the Bible tells us:

> God clearly shows and proves His own love for us, by the fact that while we were still sinners, Christ died for us.
>
> *Romans 5:8, AMP*

It is sin consciousness that is the Christian's greatest problem. The sin problem has already been dealt but, when we are ignorant of this truth, we will continue to struggle with sin, and we will have to keep confessing our sins when we err. But the truth is that the blood of Jesus is constantly speaking better things on our behalf. What are the "better things" that His blood is speaking on your behalf? The list is so long that there is no end to it; the following are just a few examples.

- You are forgiven and made righteous in Christ
- You are highly loved
- You are blessed in Christ
- You are more than a conqueror in Christ
- You are the salt of the earth and the light of the world

Declare positively that the blood of Jesus is speaking on your behalf. *Hebrews 12:24* serves as a constant reminder to you and Satan and all of heaven that the full price has been paid. Your declaration must tie in with what Jesus is saying about you. He cannot be saying you are forgiven, and you continue to feel guilty. This has nothing to do with feelings. You don't need to feel righteous to be righteous. Righteousness is a gift: just receive it by faith and enjoy it without an apologetic attitude.

You are no longer a poor, wretched sinner. You have been bought with the precious blood of Jesus. All He expects us to do is to glorify Him with our bodies, which now belong to Him. We are no longer our own (*1 Corinthians 6:19; 1 Peter 1:18-19*). We are His property. If you are His property, why worry about your life? When someone owns something, does he not take care of it? Because Jesus owns you, it is His responsibility to take care of you. We can live this life victoriously because of the blood of Jesus (*Revelation 12:11*).

Remember the hymn, "There is Power in the Blood"? Why not take time to sing it out with all your heart?

> *Would you be free from the burden of sin?*
> *There's power in the blood, power in the blood...*
> *There is power, power, wonder-working power*
> *In the precious blood of the Lamb.*

When you come to the end of your song, declare confidently:

BECAUSE I BELONG TO JESUS, HIS BLOOD SPEAKS BETTER THINGS ON MY BEHALF!

Because my God is for me, nothing and no one shall be against me

What shall we then say to these things? If God be for us, who can be against us?

Romans 8:31

Have you ever felt like everyone was against you? Ever felt like all the odds were stacked against you? Or ever felt like nothing was working out in your life? I am certain that we have all had moments when we felt like the whole world was against us. Certainly, it can be awful to feel like no one is on your side. In such moments, people who are not in Christ often resort to suicide as their only way out.

Companionship is one of our greatest needs. But, while human company can be helpful, God's companionship is the best. Commenting on *Romans 8:31*, Adam Clarke had this to say[5]:

> If God be for us, who can be against us? He who is infinitely wise has undertaken to direct us: He who is infinitely powerful has undertaken to protect us: He who is infinitely good has undertaken to save us. What cunning, strength, or malice, can prevail against his wisdom, power, and goodness? None. Therefore we are safe who love God; and not only shall sustain no essential damage by the persecutions of ungodly men, but even these things work together for our good.

---

[5] In his *Commentary on the Bible* (originally published in 8 volumes, 1810-26)

God is fully for us! This knowledge alone should give rise to celebration in honour of our great heavenly Daddy! It was thanks to this knowledge that the Hebrew boys—Shadrach, Meshach and Abednego—were able to resist King Nebuchadnezzar's command to bow down and worship the golden image he had erected (see *Daniel chapter 3*). It was this same knowledge that catapulted Daniel to go against the decree of king Darius, that all prayers should be addressed to the king and no one else (see *Daniel 6*). These are good examples for us to emulate.

These guys stood firm and God delivered them—proving that, if God is truly for us, nothing and no one can be against us. Not even fire heated seven times hotter or a den of lions. However, if God is against you, who can protect you? No court, human institution or power can defend you.

For God to be for you, you must first of all choose to be for Him. We choose Him because He has graciously chosen us first; this is what He says to us:

> You did not choose Me, but I chose you and appointed you that you should go and bear fruit, and that your fruit should remain, that whatever you ask the Father in My name He may give you.
>
> *John 15:16, NKJV*

How do you choose God? How do you ensure that God is for you? It is not by joining a church or by trying to do good deeds; all our righteous acts are like filthy rags in the eyes of God (*Isaiah 64:6*). No amount of good works can make you right with God or take you to heaven or ensure that God will stand by you always, but all you need is faith in the finished work of Christ on the cross. We are saved by the grace of God through faith (*Ephesians 2:8-9*). If you have never asked Jesus into your life, do it now (*Revelation 3:20*).

You don't need to wait for a crisis before you start seeking God. Seek Him while He may be found (*Isaiah 55:6-7*). Sad to say, some people think about God only when things go wrong. When they are "enjoying life", they have no time for God; but, when life goes awry, suddenly they see the need for God. Don't be like that. Trust in the Lord with all your heart and lean not on your own understanding, in all your ways acknowledge Him and He will make your paths straight (*Proverbs 3:5-6*). He will defend you when the time comes.

Daniel sought God regularly and that was why, when the time of testing came, he was able to stand his ground. No matter what your challenges are, if you have sincerely trusted Jesus, He is for you. Nothing and nobody shall be able to stand against you. You are more than a conqueror—no room for fear! As Paul went on to say, in his Epistle to the Romans:

> Who shall separate us from the love of Christ? Shall tribulation, or distress, or persecution, or famine, or nakedness, or peril, or sword?
>
> As it is written, for thy sake we are killed all the day long; we are accounted as sheep for the slaughter.
>
> Nay, in all these things we are more than conquerors through him that loved us.
>
> For I am persuaded, that neither death, nor life, nor angels, nor principalities, nor powers, nor things present, nor things to come, nor height, nor depth, nor any other creature, shall be able to separate us from the love of God, which is in Christ Jesus our Lord.
>
> *Romans 8:35-39*

Based on the above, you who are in Christ can declare boldly:

BECAUSE MY GOD IS FOR ME, NOTHING AND NO ONE SHALL BE AGAINST ME, IN THE NAME OF JESUS!

I am a success because I live by faith and not by sight

Now faith is the substance of things hoped for, the evidence of things not seen.

Hebrews 11:1

For we walk by faith, not by sight.

2 Corinthians 5:7

Living by faith is living according to God's Word. What is it you are believing God for? Find out what His Word says about it, and choose to stand on His Word until you see your miracle. You cannot stand on the Word of God and fail. By His grace, I have stood upon His Word and seen miracles in my life—healing, provision, protection, deliverance and empowerment.

You too can experience the joy of standing on God's Word and seeing it work. That is what faith is all about. Faith is the currency we live by in the Kingdom of God. Without it, you cannot obtain anything from God's Kingdom. It is the cable that connects us to God's unlimited resources:

> By faith we understand that the worlds were framed by the word of God, so that the things which are seen were not made of things which are visible.
>
> *Hebrews 11:3, NKJV*

Because God is spiritual reality, the substance of His Word is spiritual reality. He is the God who "gives life to the dead and calls into being that which does not exist" (*Romans 4:17, AMP*).

The spiritual is more real than the physical. All that we see in the physical is the product of what is not seen—the spiritual. As it says in *2 Corinthians 4:18*, "the things which are seen are temporal; but the things which are not seen are eternal".

Man is a spirit being, created to be and to function like his Creator (*Genesis 1:27*). But because of sin, man has forgotten his real identity—that he is a spirit, has a soul and lives in a body. Because you are a spirit, it is your spirit that is to exercise control or dominion over your soul, body and environment. For your spirit to exercise control over your soul, body and environment, however, it must first be empowered. The fuel that empowers your spirit is God's Word; as it says in *Romans 10:17*, "So then faith cometh by hearing, and hearing by the word of God."

The force derived from the intake of God's Word and applied to life's circumstances is what we call faith. When we get born again, God gives us a certain measure of faith (*Romans 12:3*), but that faith must be developed. The more we take in God's Word and apply it in our lives and see results, the more we are encouraged to take God at His word.

Some are blessed with the gift of faith. They have the capacity to believe God against all odds. They refuse to take no for an answer and strongly believe that, if God has said it, He will bring it to pass. Such faith was demonstrated by Abraham (*Genesis 15:1-6; 21:1-7; 22:1-14*), Elijah (*1 Kings chapter 18*), and many others in the Bible as well as in our present day.

It was said of Abraham that, despite facing "the fact that his body was as good as dead—since he was about a hundred years old—and that Sarah's womb was also dead", he did not weaken in his faith regarding God's promise to him to bless him with a child; but he "was strengthened in his faith and gave glory to God, being fully persuaded that God had power to do what he had promised" (*Romans 4:19-21, NIV*).

But without faith it is impossible to please Him, for he who comes to God must believe that He is, and that He is a rewarder of those who diligently seek Him.

Hebrews 11:6, NKJV

For God to be pleased with our faith, we need to develop the qualities of faith exemplified by Abraham and others like him. This involves taking our focus off our physical circumstances (*Romans 4:19*) and giving glory to God with unwavering faith (*Romans 4:20*), steadfastly believing that He will fulfill His promises (*Romans 4:21*). We can even reach out to touch Him, as did the woman with the issue of blood (*Mark 5:25-34*).

The enemy wants you to live by sight, not by faith. You must refuse to give in to his tricks. The four men carrying their paralyzed friend refused to give in to the obstacle before them. To get him past the crowds, they had to lower him from the rooftop, and their friend finally got his healing (*Mark 2:1-12*). Blind Bartimaeus is another case in point: he did not allow the crowd to stop him from getting his miracle (*Mark 10:46-52*). From these examples, it is clear that faith is action. *James 2:17* says it all: faith without works is dead.

George Müller's life story is an inspiring testimony of what can be accomplished when one lives by faith in God alone. Müller set up and ran orphanages that, in the course of his lifetime, provided for over 10,000 orphans. He never asked anyone for money but instead trusted God to provide for him and his orphans—and God never failed to do so. This is not to say that asking from people shows lack of faith on our part; but, every move we make, we must be led by God's Spirit and then we can be sure to see success (*Romans 8:14*).

Be inspired by all these examples of faith to declare:

I AM A SUCCESS BECAUSE I LIVE BY FAITH AND NOT BY SIGHT!

DAY 28—MORNING

Because of the blood of Jesus, I am the righteousness of God

God made him who had no sin to be sin for us, so that in him we might become the righteousness of God.

2 Corinthians 5:21, NIV

The story is told of a man who committed a crime and was sentenced to death. Just as he was about to be publicly executed, a stranger happened to be passing by. The stranger, a Christian, offered to die in the place of the criminal. Of course, his offer was gladly accepted and he died willingly for a man he scarcely knew. The criminal was so moved by the stranger's self-sacrifice that he decided to pay it forward by living for Christ and serving Him too.

This is exactly what happened at the cross, when Jesus died on our behalf. We are all guilty of sin and deserving of death, but God made Jesus to be a sin-offering for us, so that we might become the righteousness of God in Christ.

But what does *righteousness* mean? The Greek word used in *2 Corinthians 5:21* is *dikaiosune*, meaning "justified"; that is, we who believe in Christ have been rendered the "justified" of the Lord. We are treated as though we have fulfilled the requirements of God's law because Christ took the punishment we deserved for our disobedience.

The moment you ask Christ into your life, you are made the righteousness of God. Before coming to Christ, we were in the red; our "righteousness accounts" were empty. But when

158

we receive Christ, our accounts are credited with His righteousness. This is not earned but received by faith alone. No amount of human effort can ever make us righteous, for all our righteousness are as filthy rags before God (*Isaiah 64:6*).

It is crucial to know that you have been made right with God through the substitutionary death of Christ on the cross. Why is this so essential? Because there is now no more condemnation for you, who walk by Christ's Spirit and not according to the flesh (*Romans 8:1*). Your life can now be filled with joy and appreciation for what God has done for you.

Without righteousness, you cannot stand before God. But, because of your faith in the finished work of Christ on your behalf, you can now approach God boldly, that you may obtain mercy and find grace to help you in your time of need (*Hebrews 4:16*). You can live boldly for Christ (*Matthew 5:13-16*), talk boldly about Him (*2 Corinthians 5:20*), and be sure heaven is your eternal home (*Matthew 5:8; Hebrews 12:14*).

Righteousness is a *gift*; after receiving it by faith, we should not try to earn it, as the foolish Galatians did (*Galatians 3:1*). We can never work to merit righteousness, but we work the works of righteousness because we *are* righteous through Christ. As Paul puts it:

> I have been crucified with Christ; it is no longer I who live, but Christ lives in me; and the life which I now live in the flesh I live by faith in the Son of God, who loved me and gave Himself for me.
>
> *Galatians 2:20, NKJV*

You need not feel righteous to be righteous. Just believe, and you shall see the glory of the Lord (*John 11:40*). Declare now:

BECAUSE OF THE BLOOD OF JESUS, I AM THE RIGHTEOUSNESS OF GOD!

Because I serve Jesus, great rewards are reserved for me

"And behold, I am coming quickly, and My reward is with Me, to give to every one according to his work."

Revelation 22:12, NKJV

Our service for God can never be in vain. According to the work we do for Him, the Lord will reward us with:

- *The crown of righteousness*
- *The crown of life*
- *The crown of glory*

Always remember this: we don't work to be saved but *because* we are saved. God gives us His righteousness free of charge, but He also gives us His grace to work out our own salvation with fear and trembling (*Philippians 2:12-13*).

At the end of his life and ministry, Paul was confident that he would be given a *crown of righteousness*:

Henceforth there is laid up for me a crown of righteousness, which the Lord, the righteous judge, shall give me at that day: and not to me only, but unto all them also that love his appearing.

2 Timothy 4:8

This crown of righteousness is the reward God gives to His children for living and serving Him in integrity. Paul was sure of obtaining it because He had served the Lord with integrity.

160

The second crown, the *crown of life*, is given to those who stand firm in their faith in the midst of great trials. As you stand for Jesus, He will also stand with you—as he stood with Shadrach, Meshach and Abednego in the fiery furnace (see *Daniel chapter 3*). He will reward you for your faithfulness:

> Blessed is the one who perseveres under trial because, having stood the test, that person will receive the crown of life that the Lord has promised to those who love him.
>
> *James 1:12, NIV*

> Fear none of those things which thou shalt suffer: behold, the devil shall cast some of you into prison... and ye shall have tribulation... be thou faithful unto death, and I will give thee a crown of life.
>
> *Revelation 2:10*

The third crown, the *crown of glory*, is given for faithful service to Jesus:

> Be shepherds of God's flock that is under your care, watching over them—not because you must, but because you are willing, as God wants you to be; not pursuing dishonest gain, but eager to serve; not lording it over those entrusted to you, but being examples to the flock. And when the Chief Shepherd appears, you will receive the crown of glory that will never fade away.
>
> *1 Peter 5:2-4, NIV*

Given these great rewards ahead of us, how are we to live our lives? Paul likens it to running a race (*1 Corinthians 9:24-27*). To win the race, we need to:

- Focus on the reward that lies ahead of us (*v. 24*)
- Be disciplined and self-controlled (*vv. 25, 27*)
- Be confident and purposeful, aiming to win (*v. 26*)
- Be wise (*vv. 26-27*)

161

Only the athletes who compete according to the rules will be rewarded. Only the perseverant and hardworking farmers will reap the fruit of their labours. Only the disciplined and dedicated soldiers will be decorated (*2 Timothy 2:1-6*).

What challenges are you going through? Are you tempted to tell a lie to get out of a difficult situation? Are you tempted to give in to immorality? Are you tempted to renounce your faith? No matter what the trial or temptation, God will always make a way for those who trust in Him. He will not allow us to be tempted beyond what we can bear (*1 Corinthians 10:13*).

How are you running the race of life? Are you doing it in the steps of Jesus, Paul and others who have won their race and received their prize? If yes, praise God. If not, wake up from your slumber and run as you ought to, as someone who wants to win. You cannot afford to do anything now that will compromise the great rewards that lie ahead of you. If you have fallen, repent and persevere in the race.

> Therefore... let us throw off everything that hinders and the sin that so easily entangles. And let us run with perseverance the race marked out for us, fixing our eyes on Jesus, the pioneer and perfecter of faith. For the joy set before him he endured the cross, scorning its shame, and sat down at the right hand of the throne of God. Consider him who endured such opposition from sinners, so that you will not grow weary and lose heart.
>
> *Hebrews 12:1-3, NIV*

As you run the race of life with faith and perseverance, continue to declare confidently:

BECAUSE I SERVE JESUS, GREAT REWARDS ARE RESERVED FOR ME!

Jesus became poor that I might be rich

For ye know the grace of our Lord Jesus Christ, that, though he was rich, yet for your sakes he became poor, that ye through his poverty might be rich.

2 Corinthians 8:9

Poverty, whether physical or spiritual, has never glorified God nor ever will. Sad to say, however, some people believe that to be poor is spiritual and to be rich is evil. "Money is the root of all evil," they declare, misquoting *1 Timothy 6:10*—when in fact what Paul was saying there was that "the *love* of money is the root of all evil".

Wealth is not evil in itself, but men make it so when they choose to worship it instead of God—when they turn away from God because of their love for money. The question Jesus poses to them is: "what shall it profit a man, if he shall gain the whole world, and lose his own soul?" (*Mark 8:36*).

The greatest riches are spiritual riches. To have Christ as your Saviour and Lord is to be rich in every sense, because in Christ are hidden all the riches of God (*Colossians 2:2-3*). Not to have Christ Jesus is to be the poorest and most miserable person in this life and in the life to come.

There are many people who do not know Christ but have acquired much worldly wealth: some through genuine hard work, others through crooked means. But any riches gotten apart from Christ can never really satisfy, because the Prince of Peace is missing. These people might appear to be happy;

but within, "all is vanity and vexation of spirit," as Solomon, the richest man who ever lived, once said (*Ecclesiastes 1:14*). Moreover, all their wealth will be handed over to the godly:

> To the person who pleases him, God gives wisdom, knowledge and happiness, but to the sinner he gives the task of gathering and storing up wealth to hand it over to the one who pleases God.
>
> *Ecclesiastes 2:26, NIV*

The truth is that God wants His children to be rich in every way, so that they can live well and be a blessing to others (*Genesis 12:1-3*). So why are many Christians still poor? The answer is that the root of material poverty is spiritual poverty. All the riches that Jesus died to purchase for us are available, but there are conditions we need to fulfill to gain access to them.

First, we must understand that the greatest riches are spiritual riches. We were once spiritually poor because our sins rendered us spiritually poor. Because of sin, we lost the creative ability God had given us. We lost His favour. But, when Jesus took our sins upon Himself on the cross, he removed the barrier between us and God. When we place our faith in Jesus, God's favor is restored to us and we have access to all His resources.

To benefit from the riches Christ purchased for us, we need to depend on God's power to get wealth. As His children, we can call on Him to give us creative power to generate wealth (*Deuteronomy 8:18*). He can show you the kind of business to invest in. He can reveal to you an invention that will bless the world and, through that, produce wealth for you. He has already done this for many of His children.

Secondly, God can also give us seed to sow, through which we can become rich (*2 Corinthians 9:10-11*). God gives different kinds of seed; the kind of seed we sow will also determine our harvest. What we sow is what we will reap.

We need to sow in good ground and with the right attitude, and we need to sow qualitatively as well as quantitatively, if we are expecting to reap a rich harvest. When we talk of good ground, we are talking of sowing where God's heart is—such as salvation of souls, prison ministries, and ministry to the poor and needy. Here is what Paul had to say about sowing the seeds God gives us:

> Remember this: Whoever sows sparingly will also reap sparingly, and whoever sows generously will also reap generously. Each of you should give what you have decided in your heart to give, not reluctantly or under compulsion, for God loves a cheerful giver.
>
> *2 Corinthians 9:6-7, NIV*

Jesus became poor that you might be rich by knowing Him, following His principles, and becoming a blessing to others. Paul exhorts us to support the weak and remember the words of our Lord, for He has said, "It is more blessed to give than to receive" (*Acts 20:35, NKJV*).

We are blessed to bless. The more we bless others, the more we will experience the blessings of God in our lives. With this in mind, you can declare with confidence:

JESUS BECAME POOR THAT I MIGHT BE RICH!

Because I hunger and thirst for righteousness, I shall be filled

Blessed are those who hunger and thirst for righteousness, for they shall be filled.

Matthew 5:6, NKJV

Righteousness is at the very core of who God is and all that He does. If we desire to live and act righteously like Him—and we should, being His children—He has promised that He will grant us the grace to do so. Isn't this wonderful?

God never wastes His resources on those who are not hungry for them—just as it is wasteful to give food to someone who is not hungry and will simply throw it away. What this tells us is that it's all up to us: how far we will progress spiritually depends on how much we desire the things of God.

How strong is your desire for the things of God? Many a time, we get so caught up with the things of the world that we no longer hunger for the things of God. Instead, we hunger for things to satisfy us physically, like food, movies, parties or sex.

How can we stoke our hunger for the things of God? Here are some ways:

- Pray and fast
- Read and meditate on God's Word
- Participate in Christian meetings and fellowships
- Watch Christian movies
- Listen to Christian music

- Read Christian literature
- Attend spiritual retreats, camps and conventions

As we devote ourselves to seeking God with all our hearts, we have His promise that we will find Him (*Jeremiah 29:12-14*). In fact, God is more eager to fill us than we are to be filled. He tells those who hunger and thirst after Him:

> "I will pour water on him who is thirsty, and floods on the dry ground; I will pour My Spirit on your descendants, and My blessing on your offspring; They will spring up among the grass, like willows by the watercourses. One will say, 'I am the LORD's'; another will call himself by the name of Jacob; another will write with his hand, 'The LORD's,' and name himself by the name of Israel."
>
> *Isaiah 44:3-5, NKJV*

How do you feel when you are very hungry and you finally get to eat a good meal? Of course, you will be so energized that you can even sing and dance and just be merry! Fortified by the food, you will be able to work harder and do more.

Just as your body is satisfied when you have eaten your fill, your spirit will also be satisfied when God fills you, and you will be empowered to live joyously and serve Him better. The stronger your hunger for God, the more you will be filled. As long as we live, we can never have enough of God; the more we are filled, the more we still want of Him, because God is as inexhaustible as the ocean.

Not to hunger for God is to choose death. The answers to all your questions are found in your hunger and thirst. The solution to every one of your problems is in your hunger and thirst. For God has assured us, "Call to Me, and I will answer you, and show you great and mighty things, which you do not know" (*Jeremiah 33:3, NKJV*).

David stands out as the perfect example of someone who hungered after God. *Psalm 63:1-2*, composed by him, says it all:

> O God, thou art my God; early will I seek thee: my soul thirsteth for thee, my flesh longeth for thee in a dry and thirsty land, where no water is;
>
> To see thy power and thy glory, so as I have seen thee in the sanctuary.

God called David a man after His own heart (*Acts 13:22*) and always showed up when David called to Him. In *Psalm 34:4*, David testified to God's faithfulness, saying, "I sought the LORD, and he heard me, and delivered me from all my fears."

To be filled with God is not only to be blessed personally, but it is to become a source of blessing to others too. Thanks to David's incessant hunger and thirst for God, not only was he blessed, but Israel also enjoyed peace and prosperity under him—because God gave King David numerous victories over Israel's enemies.

Pray that God will increase your hunger and thirst for Him, so that you too may go from glory to glory (*2 Corinthians 3:18*) and be a blessing to others as well.

With this in mind, declare constantly:

BECAUSE I HUNGER AND THIRST FOR RIGHTEOUSNESS, I SHALL BE FILLED!

Jesus came to destroy the works of the devil in my life

When people do what is right, it shows that they are righteous, even as Christ is righteous. But when people keep on sinning, it shows that they belong to the devil, who has been sinning since the beginning. But the Son of God came to destroy the works of the devil.

1 John 3:7-8, NLT

This is another truth that needs to be hammered into your spirit: *Jesus has destroyed the works of the devil in your life; you are no longer a slave to sin.* If you still find yourself dominated by sin, it is an indication that you have not taken hold of this truth and this truth has not taken hold of you.
For, as Paul puts it, "We are those who have died to sin; how can we live in it any longer?" (*Romans 6:2, NIV*)

The works of the devil are numerous, enslaving many in sin. Paul listed some of them in his letter to the Galatians, with a warning that such works of darkness would prevent God's children from enjoying His best for them:

When you follow the desires of your sinful nature, the results are very clear: sexual immorality, impurity, lustful pleasures, idolatry, sorcery, hostility, quarreling, jealousy, outbursts of anger, selfish ambition, dissension, division, envy, drunkenness, wild parties, and other sins like these.

169

Let me tell you again, as I have before, that anyone living that sort of life will not inherit the Kingdom of God.

Galatians 5:19-21, NLT

When Adam and Eve sinned, all of creation became slaves in the devil's kingdom. No one was able to resist the devil before Christ came. In spite of all of God's efforts to free man from sin, he remained a perpetual slave. The Ten Commandments could not help him. The sacrifices of animals could not free man from an evil conscience but were a constant reminder of his slavery to sin.

Because of God's love for us, He decided to destroy the works of darkness that were enslaving us. Man fell in a garden —the Garden of Eden—but deliverance also came through a garden—the Garden of Gethsemane, where Jesus offered Himself up for us, to free us from slavery to the devil:

God demonstrates His own love toward us, in that while we were still sinners, Christ died for us.

Romans 5:8, NKJV

When you were dead in your sins and in the uncircumcision of your flesh (worldliness, manner of life), God made you alive together with Christ, having [freely] forgiven us all our sins, having canceled out the certificate of debt consisting of legal demands [which were in force] against us and which were hostile to us. And this certificate He has set aside and completely removed by nailing it to the cross.

When He had disarmed the rulers and authorities [those supernatural forces of evil operating against us], He made a public example of them [exhibiting them as captives in His triumphal procession], having triumphed over them through the cross.

Colossians 2:13-15, AMP

Now that you have been freed, how are you to live? How are you using your freedom in Christ? Because Jesus paid it all for me, can I now live any old way I like? Paul asked this same question too, and this is how he answered it:

> Well then, shall we keep on sinning so that God can keep on showing us more and more kindness and forgiveness?
>
> Of course not! Should we keep on sinning when we don't have to? For sin's power over us was broken when we became Christians and were baptized to become a part of Jesus Christ; through his death the power of your sinful nature was shattered.
>
> *Romans 6:1-3, TLB*

Now that Jesus has freed you, you are called to live a life of righteousness. You are married to righteousness. Paul spoke of the offspring that should result from this union with righteousness: "But when the Holy Spirit controls our lives, he will produce this kind of fruit in us: love, joy, peace, patience, kindness, goodness, faithfulness, gentleness and self-control" (*Galatians 5:22-23, TLB*).

Even if you have stumbled and fallen, ask God for forgiveness, get up and keep going. Because Jesus has freed you from the works of the devil, you are now an agent of liberation in the hands of God. Allow God to use you to preach the gospel of liberation to others, so that they too shall know the Truth, and the Truth shall set them free (*John 8:32*).

John 8:36 tells us, "If the Son therefore shall make you free, ye shall be free indeed." Believe that you have been set free, and walk as one who has been set free for the glory of God, declaring this with confidence:

JESUS CAME TO DESTROY THE WORKS OF THE DEVIL IN MY LIFE!

Because I belong to God's Kingdom, I manifest the power of His Kingdom

For the kingdom of God is not in word, but in power.

1 Corinthians 4:20

The power of God is what distinguishes His children from those who do not belong to Him. It is not enough to say that you have been born again. Something must distinguish you from those who are not part of God's Kingdom.

God's power is manifested in various ways, the first and greatest of which is the way He transforms hearts and lives. When you come to Jesus, He begins a work of transformation in you that no one else can accomplish. He changes liars and thieves into honest and dependable people. He changes the cruel and callous into kind and caring people. He changes the stingy and the selfish into generous and loving people.

He also changes people's status. The poor He raises to prosperity. The sick are healed. The oppressed are delivered. The childless become fruitful. The lame walk. The blind see, and the dead are raised to life. These transformations were manifested in Jesus' ministry as a confirmation that the Kingdom of God had come. He has assured us that anyone who believes in Him shall be able to do what He has done and even greater works than these (*John 14:12*). How many of these greater works have you already done?

Even if you have already manifested all of these greater works in your life, God is able to do more. He wants to demonstrate His power in every area of your life, in order to put the enemy to shame and draw men to Himself. To be able to manifest God's power, however, you need to:

- Desire to experience and manifest the power of God (*1 Corinthians 14:1*)

- Exercise faith, believing that you carry His power and that you can manifest it (*Hebrews 11:6*)

- Draw upon the power of praise and worship (*Psalm 22:3*)

- Walk in sanctification (*Matthew 5:8; Romans 12:1-2*)

It was said of the apostle Peter that people even carried their sick out into the streets so that, when he passed by, his shadow might fall on them with healing power (*Acts 5:15*). And of the apostle Paul, the writer of Acts had this to say:

> God did extraordinary miracles through Paul, so that even handkerchiefs and aprons that had touched him were taken to the sick, and their illnesses were cured and the evil spirits left them.
>
> *Acts 19:11-12, NIV*

When was the last time your shadow or handkerchief healed or delivered someone? Maybe recently? Or maybe not. No matter what you have accomplished in the past, you can do more. These guys were just like us. Of Elijah it was said:

> Elias was a man subject to like passions as we are, and he prayed earnestly that it might not rain: and it rained not on the earth by the space of three years and six months.
>
> And he prayed again, and the heaven gave rain, and the earth brought forth her fruit.
>
> *James 5:17-18*

173

The greatest power of the Kingdom that I have experienced in my life has been the power of transformation. Before coming to Christ, I was a slave to sinful habits like masturbation, fornication, stealing, cheating and lying. When I sincerely received Christ, all those enslavements became a thing of the past. Now I am free to walk in the righteousness of Christ.

In Paul's day, some guys were going around, making empty boasts and claiming to be apostles like him. Paul told them he was going to check on their authenticity, whether they were genuine—as testified by their works—or just noise makers. It was in line with this that he declared that "the kingdom of God is not in word, but in power" (*1 Corinthians 4:19-20*).

Satan has also tried at times to "manifest" power, but his power is fake. Whatever God does, he tries to imitate in order to draw men to his side. When God sent Moses to free Israel from slavery in Egypt, Pharaoh's magicians—who drew their power from demonic sources—were no match against the power of God (*Exodus 7:10-12*). They all failed because, when a weaker power meets a stronger power, the weaker power has no choice but to bow down to the superior power.

In the New Testament, we also find a weaker power bowing down to a stronger one. Simon the sorcerer used to mesmerize the Samaritans with his magic—until Philip the Evangelist showed up and proved to the people and Simon himself that God's power is the SUPERIOR DIVINE POWER (*Acts 8:5-25*). Therefore, do not allow the devil to intimidate you. Greater is He that is in you than he that is in the world (*1 John 4:4*).

Strongly desire to manifest God's power in your life more than ever before, always declaring in confidence:

BECAUSE I BELONG TO GOD'S KINGDOM, I MANIFEST THE POWER OF HIS KINGDOM!

By Jesus' stripes, I have been healed

But He was wounded for our transgressions, He was bruised for our iniquities; the chastisement for our peace was upon Him, and by His stripes we are healed.

Isaiah 53:5, NKJV

Who his own self bare our sins in his own body on the tree, that we, being dead to sins, should live unto righteousness: by whose stripes ye were healed.

1 Peter 2:24

Sickness, whether spiritual or physical, is not part of God's kingdom. There is no sickness in Heaven at all. Here on earth, physical sickness is a product of spiritual sickness, but Jesus' death and resurrection has set us free from both. He paid for our total liberation, including freedom from physical sickness. Why then should you be a slave to sickness any longer?

Why should you suffer for what Jesus has already suffered for you? Why carry a load that Jesus has already carried for you? I am not saying that you will never fall sick. But, whenever you fall sick, that is your opportunity to invoke the healing power of Jesus.

Doctors treat patients, but Jesus alone heals them. It is not a sin to see a doctor or use medication, but many people tend to forget that healing is already available through Jesus' death. The first thing that comes to their mind is not prayer for healing. What comes to their mind first is medication.

Many people spend all their hard-earned money on medication, trying to get well. This is the work of the devil: your money is not meant to be spent on medication but to help further God's Kingdom on earth.

Some people even have illnesses troubling them for so long that they have taken to calling it "their" sickness: "That's my headache" ... "That's my arthritis" .... "That's my cough," they say. You should never personalize any ailment, for the power of life and death is in the tongue (*Proverbs 18:21*).

Behind most infirmities is a devil (*Luke 13:16*). So, if your health is attacked, identify the devil that is behind the ailment: call it by its name and command it in the Name of Jesus to leave you. No matter how debilitating it is, no sickness is above the Name of Jesus; for, at the Name of Jesus, every knee must bow, in heaven and on earth and under the earth (*Philippians 2:10*). The Name of Jesus is above cancer, HIV, AIDS, diabetes, asthma, blindness and every other infirmity.

If the illness is trying to be stubborn and refuses to leave you, you too become just as stubborn and refuse to take no for an answer (*Luke 10:19; 1 Peter 5:8-9*). At times, you may also need to call for support:

> Are any of you sick? You should call for the elders of the church to come and pray over you, anointing you with oil in the name of the Lord. Such a prayer offered in faith will heal the sick, and the Lord will make you well. And if you have committed any sins, you will be forgiven.
>
> *James 5:14-15, NLT*

We cannot afford to allow sickness to oppress us and keep us from serving God or fulfilling our destiny. The good news is that all we need for life and godliness—including healing—is already available in Christ (*2 Peter 1:3-4*).

By Jesus' stripes, we can receive healing in every area of our lives—physically and emotionally, as well as spiritually. We can enjoy healthy relationships with our family and others, healthy finances, healthy work-life balances, and healthy growth in our academic and professional lives.

It is our responsibility to receive that which is ours by faith; Jesus called it "the children's bread" (*Matthew 15:26*). Are you presently struggling with any health issues? Is there any area of your life that is sick? If yes, here is a prayer you can say—and receive your healing by faith:

> *In the Name of Jesus, I speak healing into every area of my life. You, spirit of infirmity that is attacking my body, my soul, my spirit, my relationships, my family, my finances, my studies, and my work, be cast out of my life into the deepest of oceans! In the Name of Jesus Christ!*

Now that you have received your healing, remember that whatever God has given us requires appreciation and maintenance. To continue to enjoy good physical health, we need to eat nutritious meals and get enough sleep and exercise. To be spiritually strong, we need to read God's Word and spend time alone with Him every day. To maintain healthy family ties, we need to spend time with our family members. And, keeping in mind that the power of life and death is in the tongue, we need to declare boldly:

BY JESUS' STRIPES, I HAVE BEEN HEALED!

Because I am watchful, I shall not miss the Rapture

Watch therefore, for you do not know what hour your Lord is coming.

Matthew 24:42, NKJV

Heaven and Hell are real places, believe it or not! Heaven is for those who believe in Christ and are living a Christ-centered life; you might call it a *prepared* place for *prepared* persons. Hell is for the devil and those who reject Christ.

The Rapture of the Church of Jesus Christ will be a world-shaking event. It will happen when Jesus comes for His bride, the Church. The Church is not a building or a denomination or an organization, but a living organism with different parts. It is called the Body of Christ. All who believe in Christ make up this Body. They live their lives to please their Master, keeping themselves pure in anticipation of His return.

Jesus has put apostles, prophets, evangelists, pastors and teachers at the disposal of His Church (*Ephesians 4:11-13*) to prepare her for His coming. He is coming back for a Church that He has redeemed by His death on the cross:

He gave up his life for her to make her holy and clean, washed by the cleansing of God's word. He did this to present her to himself as a glorious church without a spot or wrinkle or any other blemish. Instead, she will be holy and without fault.

Ephesians 5:25-27, NLT

The worst thing that can happen to anyone who claims to believe in Christ is to miss the Rapture. This is because, after the Rapture, it is going to take exceptional grace for you to be saved. The Antichrist will take over the scene and impose his mark—the number 666—on your forehead or right hand.

If you refuse to take this mark, you will not be able to buy or sell (*Revelation 13:17-18*), and you will be subjected to the worst torture ever. But if you agree to take the mark, which signifies allegiance to the Antichrist, you will be condemned to spend eternity in the lake of fire (*Revelation 20:15*), which is a horrible place; you don't want to end up there.

The Great Tribulation will last seven years, after which Jesus will come back to earth with His bride to reign for a thousand years; and after that the Final Judgment will come, leading us into eternity. The righteous will enter into the New Jerusalem (*Revelation 3:12; 21:2*) and the sinners into everlasting damnation in the lake of fire (*Revelation 21:8*). You cannot afford to miss out on an eternal home as glorious as the New Jerusalem—God's dwelling place!

> And I saw the holy city, the new Jerusalem, coming down from God out of heaven like a bride beautifully dressed for her husband. I heard a loud shout from the throne, saying, "Look, God's home is now among his people! He will live with them, and they will be his people. God himself will be with them. He will wipe every tear from their eyes, and there will be no more death or sorrow or crying or pain. All these things are gone forever."
>
> *Revelation 21:2-4, NLT*

Jesus tells us to watch and pray and be ready at all times, for we do not know the hour of His coming. What this implies is that we need to live like the wise virgins in *Matthew 25:1-13*, who acted diligently to ensure they were ready for His coming.

The Bible tells us clearly that faith without works is dead (*James 2:14-26*). I need to demonstrate my faith in Christ by living a life that honors Him, acting diligently and making the most of every opportunity to win souls for His Kingdom, and doing good to my fellowmen. This has eternal consequences:

> "But when I, the Messiah, shall come in my glory, and all the angels with me, then I shall sit upon my throne of glory. And all the nations shall be gathered before me. And I will separate the people as a shepherd separates the sheep from the goats, and place the sheep at my right hand, and the goats at my left.
>
> "Then I, the King, shall say to those at my right, 'Come, blessed of my Father, into the Kingdom prepared for you from the founding of the world. For I was hungry and you fed me; I was thirsty and you gave me water; I was a stranger and you invited me into your homes; naked and you clothed me; sick and in prison, and you visited me.'
>
> "Then these righteous ones will reply, 'Sir, when did we ever see you hungry and feed you? Or thirsty and give you anything to drink? Or a stranger, and help you? Or naked, and clothe you? When did we ever see you sick or in prison, and visit you?'
>
> "And I, the King, will tell them, 'When you did it to these my brothers, you were doing it to me!'
>
> *Matthew 25:31-40, TLB*

If the rapture happens now, would you be able to make it? If yes, praise God! If no, you need to make things right with God now. I encourage you to meditate on *Acts 2:36-39*. If you are living your life for Christ, you can declare with confidence:

BECAUSE I AM WATCHFUL, I SHALL NOT MISS THE RAPTURE!

180

* 9 7 8 9 8 1 1 4 3 6 6 9 7 *